EXAMINING 15 PRO-CHOICE CLAIMS

What Do Facts & Common Sense Tell Us?

PRO-CHOICE

OR

PRO-LIFE?

RANDY ALCORN

WITH STEPHANIE ANDERSON

With thanks to Kathy Norquist,
Doreen Button, Chelsea Dudley,
and Larry Gadbaugh

CONTENTS

INTRODUCTION

Why talk about abortion?

The relentless debate between the pro-choice and pro-life positions is one of the most divisive and perplexing in American history, and for that matter in *world* history. Many of us have seen what happens when those who have strong opinions one way or the other try to discuss the abortion issue. Sometimes the discussions are rational and productive. Most of the time they rapidly become heated and accusatory, generating far more heat than light.

This issue divides people not only on the streets and in workplaces, but also in homes and churches. There are few matters so personal as our decisions about sex, pregnancy, parenting, and our health. So while abortion is difficult to talk about, it's important to provide accurate information and a context in which that information can be discussed.

Are pro-choice and pro-life interactions destined to be dialogues of the deaf? Or can proponents actually meet on common ground? I believe that both views have at least four points in common.

1) We all have access to the same large body of empirical data—scientific and

psychological evidence that we need not and should not deny.

2) We share the ability (if we let go of prejudices) to be logical and rational in applying scientific truth.

3) We share a sense of morality and the value of justice, fairness, and compassion to others.

4) We share a common desire to support the dignity of individuals, especially women and others who have suffered oppression.

In our increasingly polarized culture, learning how to listen to those we differ with will make us and our community better.

Aren't We All Both Pro-Choice and Pro-Life?

There's something strange about the terminology in this debate, isn't there? After all, aren't we *all* pro-choice? And aren't we *all* pro-life?

The answer to both questions is yes!

This sounds simplistic, and I'm certainly not presuming to solve the disagreement with semantics. But if asked, "Are you pro-slavery or anti-slavery?" or "Are you pro-kidnapping or anti-kidnapping?" wouldn't you expect people to give a clear answer? Don't the questions themselves make the issues at stake self-evident?

What do the words pro-life and pro-choice even *mean*? The words themselves are misleading. The opposites are *anti-life* and *anti-choice*. But do pro-choice people hate life? No. Do pro-life people hate choice? Of course not.

Pro-choice people don't believe parents have the right to choose killing their six-year-olds or teenagers, that husbands have the right to choose killing their wives, or that anyone has the right to choose to treat someone unjustly based on their skin color. Pro-choice parents love their children, and they would likely jump into a pool to save the life of their neighbor's child, or a stranger's, just as a pro-life person would. If you don't think they are pro-life in most every area, you'd find out otherwise if you threatened the lives of those they love!

Pro-life advocates daily and repeatedly, moment by moment, practice their right to choose. They choose Mexican or Chinese food over Thai or Italian food with no qualms and don't condemn anyone for making a different choice. They choose public school, private school, or homeschool for their children, and they choose where they want to live or what they watch on TV, exactly like pro-choice advocates do. In fact, even when they oppose the morality of certain choices, such as watching sexually explicit television programs or having sex outside marriage, very few of them try to prevent those actions. If you don't believe they are pro-choice in most every area, just try to take away their freedom to choose!

Since most of us are nearly always pro-choice and nearly always pro-life, maybe we can find some common ground and therefore some basis for constructive dialogue. If we *all* believe in life and we *all* believe in choice, maybe we can listen to each other concerning this difficult thing called abortion.

Abortion in America

There are few issues as impactful and consequential for our personal lives and communities as abortion. After all, abortion is America's most frequently performed surgery on women. The Guttmacher Institute, a polling agency originally affiliated with Planned Parenthood, reports that 18 percent of pregnancies in 2017 ended in surgical abortion.[1] That year there were 862,320 abortions, down 7% from 926,190 abortions in 2014.[2] The latest statistics available show that globally, one in four pregnancies end in abortion.[3]

Whether or not they realize it, nearly every family, peer group, and church has, at some level, been touched by abortion.

The stakes in this issue are extraordinarily high. If the pro-choice position is correct, the freedom to choose abortion is a basic civil right, and no one should be able to restrict that right. If the pro-life position is correct, abortion causes approximately 2,400 infant casualties *every day* in America (not counting chemical abortions). That's nearly as many victims as the total number of lives lost in the September 11, 2001 destruction of the World Trade Center.

The statistics reflect America's split on this issue. A 2019 Gallup poll indicated that 49 percent of Americans identify as pro-life, and 46 percent identify as pro-choice. They noted that "The division between Americans identifying as pro-life and pro-choice has been particularly close in recent years. Since 2007, the percentages identifying as pro-choice and pro-life have each averaged 47% and the figures have varied by no more than five points in either direction." Still, 53 percent of American adults say abortion should be legal "only under certain circumstances," while 25 percent say it should be legal with absolutely no restrictions.[4]

A Challenge to My Pro-Choice (and Pro-Life) Readers

If you're pro-choice and reading this small book, I'm glad. I trust this means you have an open mind. If the pro-life side proves to be as senseless and irrational as you thought it was, you can give it the firsthand rejection it deserves. But if it proves to be more sensible than you expected, then I encourage you to rethink your position.

Is this book biased? Of course. Every argument, every presentation of thought, reflects a bias, so rather than pretending to be entirely transparent, let's all be self-aware. I am biased toward racial equality and against looting. You probably are too, but that doesn't mean we don't have good reasons for our biases. The question is not bias; the question is, which bias is most solidly based on the facts? Which bias is the most reasonable and defensible?

I have honestly tried to be fair. I have tried not to quote people out of context, and I have sought to accurately represent the pro-choice position. I know and like many who support reproductive choice. I have listened to them, read their books, and watched their videos. (I think it's fair to say I've studied the pro-choice arguments far more than most pro-choice people have.) I do not imagine people who are pro-choice are plotting to destroy civilization. I think they honestly believe that abortion is a necessary option that is ultimately best both for women and our society.

Therefore, I don't ask anyone to accept the pro-life position without thinking. On the contrary, I ask all readers to look at the evidence and weigh it on its own merit. Set aside stereotypes of the pro-life position. Be intellectually honest and resist the temptation to be politically correct by holding to the pro-choice position even if it turns out that the evidence leads you to uncomfortable conclusions.

If you have mixed feelings about abortion, as many people do, I ask you to make these chapters part of your quest for truth. You can hear the pro-choice position anywhere—just watch TV or read the news or sit in most classrooms. But unless you read or listen to other viewpoints more widely than most people, this book may be your first exposure to the actual logical arguments for the pro-life position (not merely to pro-life sound bites that can be easily refuted). This could be your opportunity to hear and examine the actual pro-life position, not mere caricatures of it.

If you're pro-life, I also ask you to think through your position. It isn't good enough to say, "I know I'm right, but I'm not sure why." We should base our beliefs on evidence. If we're wrong on any point, by all means let's revise our position. If we're correct, we need to learn how to intelligently and graciously inform others.

Did you dismiss the viewpoint I shared that

pro-choicers are pro-life in most areas? If so, what evidence do you have to the contrary? Do you resist the idea that there is substantial common ground that should open the door for rational exchanges instead of yelling at each other or refusing to dialogue? If so, why?

I encourage pro-lifers and pro-choicers not to demonize each other. Both can tell endless tales of being treated as wicked and uncaring, when in their own thinking they are only defending the rights of others. If we have any hope of understanding and engaging with each other, let's move our dialogue beyond bumper stickers, memes, and tweets.

If abortion does *not* kill or harm people, the pro-life mentality is worse than a nuisance—it's a serious threat to women's rights and personal liberty, and it's responsible for imposing a baseless guilt on those who've had abortions. It's also a terrible waste for pro-lifers, whose time, money, and personal efforts could be far more constructively invested in helping real people with real needs.

If abortion *does* kill children and harm women, the pro-choice mentality is responsible for the deaths of over 800,000 of the smallest and most vulnerable American children each year. It would mean that since *Roe v. Wade* in 1973, over 60 million children have lost their lives through abortion.[5] It's also largely to blame for the feelings of guilt, depression, despair, and even suicidal tendencies that many women have experienced despite being assured that abortion is in their best interests.

Clearly this isn't a case where "it doesn't make

a difference who's right and who's wrong." True, if we hold firmly to either position we can't help but believe the other is doing great harm. But can we please listen carefully to the arguments on both sides? I am presenting the case for the pro-life side. You have probably heard the pro-choice side, perhaps primarily or exclusively, but if you haven't, by all means do your homework and look at that rationale. Then see how the two positions stand up against each other.

I have built this book around what I believe are fifteen major claims of the pro-choice position. I will share responses that I believe to be fact-based and rational. It's up to you to decide whether or not you agree.

"The embryo isn't a baby— it's just a product of conception and a potential life."

A woman getting an abortion relayed this conversation with her abortion clinic counselor:

"What does a three-month-old fetus look like?"

"Just a clump of cells," she answered matter-of-factly.[1]

Later this same woman viewed pictures of fetal development. She said, "When I saw that a three-month-old 'clump of cells' had fingers and toes and was a tiny perfectly formed baby, I became really hysterical. I'd been lied to and misled. I'm sure thousands of other women are being just as poorly informed and badly served."[2]

The Fetus: A Living, Functioning Organism

From a scientific standpoint, the assertion that a human embryo is merely "a clump of cells" is wholly inaccurate.

Dr. Maureen L. Condic, Assistant Professor of Neurobiology and Anatomy at the University of

Utah, challenges readers to consider the fundamental difference between a clump of living cells and an organism like an adult or an unborn child.

Dr. Condic explains that even dead bodies, for a time, contain clumps of living cells that continue to function: "Cellular life may continue for some time following the loss of integrated bodily function, but once the ability to act in a coordinated manner has been lost, 'life' cannot be restored to a corpse—no matter how 'alive' the cells composing the body may yet be."[3]

A human embryo, on the other hand, is vastly different than a corpse composed of clumps of cells. Dr. Condic writes:

> Embryos are not merely collections of human cells, but living creatures with all the properties that define any organism as distinct from a group of cells; embryos are capable of growing, maturing, maintaining a physiologic balance between various organ systems, adapting to changing circumstances, and repairing injury. Mere groups of human cells do nothing like this under any circumstances.[4]

Dr. Condic continues:

> [F]or many, it is difficult to imagine that something that looks more like a bag of marbles than a baby could possibly be a human being. Fundamentally, this argument asserts

that human life is worthy of respect depending on appearance. When plainly stated, this conclusion is quite disturbing and also quite problematic. What level of malformation are we willing to accept before we revoke the right to continued existence?[5]

Ultrasound technology has given us a window into the womb, helping people see the obvious humanity of the unborn, especially as she goes on developing. In the earliest stages after conception, the unborn child doesn't appear human to us who are used to judging humanity by what we typically see. Nevertheless, in the objective scientific sense she is every bit as human as any older child or adult. In fact, *she looks just like a human being ought to look at her stage of development.* Furthermore, as we'll see, she'll move to the next stages very quickly and will look like a baby often before her mother even knows she's pregnant.

What Happens in Early Pregnancy

The newly fertilized egg, a distinct and living organism, contains a staggering amount of genetic information, sufficient to control the individual's growth and development for his or her entire lifetime. A single thread of DNA from a human cell contains information equivalent to a library of one thousand volumes.[6] Today we know the human genome has up to three billion base pairs of DNA that influence the expression of traits in an individual cell.[7]

The cells of the new individual divide and multiply rapidly, resulting in phenomenal growth. *Growth occurs because a life exists.*

Between five and nine days after conception the new person burrows into the womb's wall for safety and nourishment. Already his or her gender can be determined by scientific means. It will be two more weeks before clearly human features are discernible and three more before they're obvious.

At just eighteen days after conception the heart is forming and eyes start to develop. By twenty-one days the heart pumps blood throughout the body. By twenty-eight days the unborn baby has budding arms and legs. By thirty days she has a brain and has multiplied in size *ten thousand times*!

By thirty-five days her mouth, ears, and nose are taking shape. At forty days the preborn child's brain waves can be recorded, and her heartbeat, which began three weeks earlier, can be detected by an ultrasonic stethoscope. By forty-two days her skeleton is formed and her brain is controlling the movement of muscles and organs.

By eight weeks hands and feet are almost perfectly formed. The nine-week baby has "already perfected a somersault, backflip and scissor kick."[8] The unborn child responds to stimulus and may already be capable of feeling pain.[9]

By ten weeks the child squints, swallows, and frowns. By eleven weeks she urinates, makes a wide variety of facial expressions including smiles.[10] By twelve weeks the child turns her feet, curling and fanning her toes, makes a fist, moves thumbs, bends wrists, and opens her mouth.[11]

All this happens in the first trimester, the first three months of life. This is no mere clump of cells! This is a living, growing human being.

"I'm Pregnant with a Product of Conception" or "I'm Carrying a Child"?

Abortion advocates and abortion clinic counselors often use dehumanizing language, especially when referring to very early pregnancies, to redirect women from thinking abortion kills a human being. But the language we use when it comes to talking about *wanted* pregnancies reveals we know better.

When have you ever heard a woman announce to friends and family, "I'm pregnant with a clump of cells"? It's always, "I'm expecting a *baby!*" No one ever responds to the news by saying, "Congratulations on your potential life!" Instead they ask, "When is your *baby* due?" A variety of women's t-shirts feature the message "Baby on board!" Have you ever seen t-shirts that say "Clump of cells/ Potential life on board"? Or even "Fetus on board"? As long as it's wanted, doesn't *everybody* recognize it's a baby?

Whenever we discuss abortion, we are always discussing the death of a preborn person, with measurable brainwaves and a discernible heartbeat. In no scientific or logical sense is he or she just "a blob of tissue" or a "clump of cells."

"Well, the fetus may be human, but it isn't a *person*."

Two ethicists wrote an article for the *Journal of Medical Ethics* arguing that doctors should be allowed to abort *newborn babies* because they're "not persons." They wrote that when "circumstances occur after birth such that they would have justified abortion, what we call after-birth abortion should be permissible." The authors admitted that "both a fetus and a newborn certainly are human beings and potential persons," but argued that "neither is a 'person' in the sense of 'subject of a moral right to life.'"[1]

Most people are naturally horrified at the idea of killing newborn babies, and the article in the *Journal of Medical Ethics* provoked a fierce public backlash. But what many people failed to realize is that the authors' argument is precisely the same argument used by abortion advocates to justify aborting babies *before* they are born. In fact, very similar arguments were used to justify terrible evils like slavery and the Holocaust, as well as the subjugation of women and the dehumanizing treatment of the disabled and mentally ill. Their rights were violated because it was sometimes said and often believed that blacks,

Jews, women, and the mentally or physically disabled "aren't people, at least not *fully*."

The argument goes like this: while the unborn child (or slave or Jew) is indeed a living human being (science clearly shows that to be the case), he or she isn't a "person," and therefore doesn't have the right to life.

But what if personhood isn't something bestowed on human beings by Ivy League professors and ethicists who favor ridding society of "undesirables" who are a drain on the rest of us? What if personhood has an inherent value that comes simply from being a member of the human race? This is what pro-lifers—and most ethicists, until recently—have believed.

What Makes Someone a Person

The Fourteenth Amendment of the U.S. Constitution says that the state shall not deprive any person of life without due process of law. When that was written, the word *human* meant the same thing as *person*. The words were interchangeable.

But in *Roe v. Wade*, the U.S. Supreme Court decision that legalized abortion in the United States, the Court was faced with a conundrum. "If the suggestion of personhood [of the unborn] is established," they admitted, "the appellant's [pro-abortion] case, of course, collapses, for the fetus's right to life is then guaranteed specifically by the [fourteenth] amendment."[2]

To solve this problem, the justices chose to abandon the historic meaning of personhood, and instead suggested that "personhood" is something different from being human. "Personhood" became something that a human being *develops* at some point, based upon some set of criteria. In the Supreme Court's case, they argued that a human fetus develops personhood at the point of "viability"—i.e. the point when a baby can live outside his mother's body.

In the years following, pro-choice advocates have made a long series of subjective and artificial distinctions based upon a wide variety of criteria to differentiate between *humans* and *persons*. They've been forced to do this because the scientific fact that life begins at conception paints the pro-choice movement into a corner. The development of advanced ultrasound and modern embryology has made it very difficult for pro-choice advocates to deny that the fetus is *human* without looking anti-scientific. Therefore, the newer strategy is to say, "OK, this is human life, but it isn't really a *person*."

But changing the meaning of words doesn't change reality. The modern concept of "personhood," redefined specifically to justify abortion, is hopelessly subjective and virtually worthless as an ethical guide. The only objective questions we can ask are these:

- "Is it human; that is, did it come from human beings?"
- "Is it a genetically unique individual?"
- "Is it alive and growing?"

If the answers are yes, then the "it" is in fact a "he" or "she," a living person, possessing rights, and deserving legal protection.

Dictionaries still define *person* as a "human being," "human individual," or "member of the human race." What makes a dog a dog is that he came from dogs. His father was a dog and his mother was a dog, and therefore he is a dog. What makes a human a human is that he *came from humans*. His father was a human and his mother was a human, so he can be nothing other than a human.

Viability: An Arbitrary Measure of Personhood

In *Roe v. Wade*, the Supreme Court defined viability—and therefore personhood—as the point when the unborn is "potentially able to live outside the mother's womb, albeit with artificial aid."[3] The critical issue as to when this point is reached is the development of the child's lungs.

But why make personhood dependent upon viability? Why not say he becomes human in the fourth week because that's when his heart beats? Or the sixth week because that's when she has brain waves? (Both are also arbitrary, yet both would eliminate the great majority of surgical abortions currently performed.)

Couldn't someone also argue that personhood begins when the unborn child first sucks his thumb or responds to light and noise? Or why not say that personhood begins when the child takes his first step or is potty trained or fully capable of taking care of himself so he's no longer a burden to his parents?

Once we decide that some human beings don't possess the right to life because of a set of subjective criteria, there's no stopping what injustices we can rationalize against those most in need of our protection.

Furthermore, viability depends not only on the child but also on the ability of our technology to save his life. What will happen when we're able to save lives at fifteen weeks or less? Will those children suddenly become human and worthy to live? Can we honestly believe that two decades ago children at twenty-one weeks of prenatal development were not people, but those born at the same age now are people simply because of improved technology?

Do Philosophy Professors Know Something the Rest of Us Don't?

Years ago Peter Singer, Princeton philosophy professor, wrote in his ethics textbook, "The life of a fetus is of no greater value than the life of a nonhuman animal at a similar level of rationality, self-consciousness, awareness, capacity to feel, etc."[4]

At the time, Singer offered pro-choice advocates emphatic intellectual and academic support of their position. He also claimed, "Since no fetus is a person, no fetus has the same claim to life as a person." He further argued that those who were once people can lose their personhood through brain damage or dementia.

Singer said, "If we compare a severely defective human infant with a nonhuman animal, a dog or a pig, for example, we will often find the nonhuman to have superior capacities, both actual and potential, for rationality, self-consciousness, communication and anything else that can plausibly be considered morally significant."[5]

Singer also suggests that individual human worth is based on nothing more than its usefulness to others: "When the death of a disabled infant will lead to the birth of another infant with better prospects of a happy life, the total amount of happiness will be greater if the disabled infant is killed. The loss of happy life for the first infant is outweighed by the gain of a happier life for the second. Therefore, if killing the hemophiliac infant has no adverse effect on others, it would, according to the total view, be right to kill him."[6]

When Singer came to teach at Princeton, he was protested by *Not Dead Yet*, a disabilities rights group. They took offense at Singer's books, which say it should be legal to kill disabled infants, as well as children and adults with severe cognitive disabilities.

Dr. Charles Hartshorne of the University of Texas at Austin echoes Singer's ethic: "Of course, an infant is not fully human.... I have little sympathy with the idea that infanticide is just another form of murder. Persons who are already functionally persons in the full sense have more important rights even than infants."[7]

Almost 72% of children murdered by their own parents were six years old or younger. And one-third of the victims were under one year of age. [8] If it's perfectly legal and acceptable to kill a child up until birth, for reasons that include personal preferences and financial welfare, why shouldn't we expect some parents to kill their children once they are born and become less convenient and more expensive? If it was perfectly fine to kill the same child months earlier, why isn't it alright to kill them now?

We cringe at stories of young parents discarding newborns in trash cans. But they're operating by the logic that parents have the same right to dispose of their inconvenient and unwanted children after birth that society said they had *before* birth. Once the child-abuse mentality grips a society, it does not restrict itself to abusing only one group of children. If preborn children aren't safe, neither are born children.

Peter Singer says, "There remains, however, the problem of the lack of any clear boundary between the newborn infant, who is clearly not a person in the ethically relevant sense, and the young child who is. In our book, *Should the Baby Live?*, my colleague Helga Kuhse and I suggested that a period of twenty-eight days after birth might be allowed before an infant is accepted as having the same right to life as others."[9]

Think of the staggering implications of the viewpoint. Singer and Kuhse, with favorable citations by many pro-choice advocates, actually proposed that children should not be declared people until some time after their birth. That way, if the parents decide to dispose of them, they wouldn't have to face legal consequences.

Like it or not, this is the natural result of pro-choice thinking. If it's acceptable to kill a child five months before birth, it's acceptable to kill her five minutes before birth. Or five minutes after birth. Or five months after birth.

Is that really the world you want you and your children and grandchildren to live and die in?

If smart and powerful people are given the right to declare that certain people with mental and physical disabilities are not people at all, and therefore have fewer rights or no rights at all, where does that logic lead? If those who cannot think do not deserve to live, what about those who think incorrectly—that is, those who disagree with the people in power? Consider how totalitarian states (where dissidents are routinely imprisoned, tortured, and executed) apply that logic.

Humanity, Not Ability, Imparts Personhood

Pro-choice advocates point out that a child aborted in the first trimester may be less than an inch or two in size, or less than an ounce or two in weight. But is size a legitimate measure of personhood? Is a professional basketball player more of a person than someone half his size? If a two-hundred-pound man loses fifty pounds, does he lose one fourth of his personhood? Scales and rulers cannot measure human nature or worth. Intuitively, we all understand the truth put so simply by Dr. Seuss in *Horton Hears a Who*: "Because, after all, a person is a person, no matter how small."[10]

Joseph Fletcher, while professor at University of Virginia, argued that an "individual" is not a "person" unless he has an IQ of at least 40, is self-aware, and has self-control, with a sense of time

21

(past, present, and future) and an ability to relate to others.[11]

But if personhood is determined by one's current capacities, then a child or adult with a mental handicap isn't a person. By the same standard, someone who is unconscious or sick or even asleep could be killed because he's not demonstrating superior intellect and skills. "But give that person time and he'll be able to function as a person." Give the baby time and so will she.

Dr. Maureen L. Condic writes:

Unless we are willing to assign "personhood" proportionate to ability (young children, for example, might be only 20 percent human, while people with myopia 95 percent), the limited abilities of prenatal humans are irrelevant to their status as human beings.[12]

Age, size, IQ, location, or stage of development are simply differences in degree, not in kind. Our kind is humanity. We are people—human beings. We possess skills in differing degrees at different stages of development. Even at maturity, our abilities and IQ levels vary. But none of these measurements make some people more human than others, do they?

Jonathan Leeman and Matthew Arbo ask readers to consider the further implications of defining personhood by ability:

All that's required to be a person is to be a member of the species. A human quite simply *is* a person, irrevocably and unqualifiedly. And thus it matters not at all whether someone is impaired, unconscious, or "viable."

Consider the flip side. If membership in the species is *not* the standard, then it falls to whoever has the most power to establish criteria for which people "are people" and which "are not people." If you possess all the guns, or all the clubs, or all the land, or a majority on the Supreme Court, you get to set the standards for who is and who is not a person. Sound frightening?[13]

Conception: The Only Objective Point of Personhood

There is only one objective point of origin for any human being, only one point at which there was not a person a moment ago, and there is now. That point is conception—which science clearly shows is the moment when a new, utterly unique human being—a *person*—comes into existence.

"Even if a fetus is a person, no person is allowed to live off the body of another person without permission."

Some pro-choice advocates argue that even if a "fetus" is actually a person, that doesn't change the fact that one person does not have the right to use the body of another person against their will (in this case, against the mother's will). Therefore, she should have the right to "evict" the fetus from her body.

In his book *Abortion Practice*, Warren Hern, one of the world's most prominent abortionists, wrote that "the relationship between the [mother] and the [baby] can be understood best as one of host and parasite."[1] He's not alone in this view. One woman, referring to the twins she was pregnant with and later aborted, wrote, "Right now it's just a parasite only living off of me."[2]

Jia Tolentino says, "If the fetus is a person, it is a person who possesses, as Sally Rooney put it in the *London Review of Books*, 'a vastly expanded set of legal rights, rights available to no other class of citizen'—the right to 'make free, non-consensual use of another living person's uterus and blood supply, and cause permanent, unwanted changes to another person's body.' In the relationship between woman and fetus, she wrote, the woman is 'granted fewer rights than a corpse.'"[3]

"Kidnapped" for Nine Months?

This line of argument is not new. Years ago, abortion-rights advocate Judith Jarvis Thomson invented an analogy that was widely quoted in pro-choice literature and debates. She compared pregnancy to a situation in which someone wakes up strapped to a famous but unconscious violinist. Imagine, Thomson says, that some group called the Society of Music Lovers has "kidnapped" you because you have a certain blood type. Now you are being forced to stay "plugged in" to the violinist's body for nine months until he is viable, or able to live on his own.

Thomson then asked what if it were not just nine months, but nine years or considerably longer? (This is a comparison to having to raise a child once he's born.) Thomson assumes that readers would find such a situation "outrageous" and would not consider it their obligation to be subjected to nine months—at least—of bondage and misery for the sake of the violinist, who is little more than a human parasite.[4]

This analogy is worth a closer examination, because it's typical of the way the abortion issue is framed by pro-choice advocates in our society. Following are four fallacies of this argument that cut to the heart of the abortion debate.

1. *An extremely high percentage of pregnancies, over 98%, are the result of sexual relations in which both partners have willingly participated.* A woman is rarely coerced or forced into pregnancy. The parallel to the Society of Music Lovers exists nowhere except in Thomson's mind. A very small number of women are in fact pregnant due to rape, and words cannot express the compassion we should have for these women. However, while Thomson's idea of most pregnant women being kidnapped and coerced is an effective emotional device, it is a distortion of reality. Can you name any entity forcing people to have sex and get pregnant?

2. *In this scenario, mother and child are pitted against each other as enemies.* The mother is at best merely a life-support system and at worst the victim of a crime. The child is a leech, a parasite unfairly taking advantage of the mother and invading her privacy. Love, compassion, and care are nowhere present. The bonding between mother and child is totally ignored. The picture of a woman waking up in a bed, strapped to a strange unconscious man is bizarre and degrading to women, whose pregnancy and motherhood are natural events.

"The violinist is artificially attached to the woman," Greg Koukl writes. "A mother's unborn baby, however, is not surgically connected, nor was it ever 'attached' to her. Instead, the baby is being produced by the mother's own body by the natural process of reproduction."[5]

In addition, those who have religious beliefs typically think there is also the supernatural presence of a Creator who has formed the child in his image, making him or her sacred, not parasitical.

3. *The child's presence during pregnancy is rarely more inconvenient than his presence after birth.* The burden of a born child is usually greater on a woman than the burden of an unborn child. Yet if the parent of a two-year-old decides that she is tired of being a parent and that no one has the right to expect her to be one any longer, society nonetheless recognizes that she has certain responsibilities toward that child. She can surrender him for foster care or adoption, but she cannot legally abuse, neglect, or kill the child. If killing the preborn child is her solution to the stresses of pregnancy, is killing not also the solution to the greater stresses of parenting a preschooler?

Greg Koukl asks, "What if the mother woke up from an accident to find herself surgically connected *to her own child*? What kind of mother would willingly cut the life-support system to her two-year-old in a situation like that? And what would we think of her if she did?"[6]

4. *Even when there is no felt obligation, there is sometimes real obligation.* If a woman is being raped or murdered, what do we think of those who make no effort to rescue her? Don't we recognize there is moral responsibility toward saving a life, even if it involves an inconvenience or risk we didn't ask for or want? Scott Klusendorf puts it this way: "We may not have the obligation to sustain strangers who are unnaturally plugged into us, but we do have a duty to sustain our own offspring."[7]

For the woman carrying a child, surely it's a significant consideration that her own mother made exactly the same sacrifice for her. Can we forget that every one of us was once this "leech," this "parasite" dependent on our mothers in order to live? Aren't you glad your mother looked at pregnancy—and looked at you—differently than these analogies?

A Symptom of a Broken Society

This argument for abortion is based in utilitarianism, the idea that whatever brings a person momentary happiness or relief is the right course of action. This is a shaky foundation for any society that hopes to be moral and just in its treatment of the weak and needy.

As Michael Spielman, founder and director of Abort73, says, "The absolute dependence of unborn children has become the rationale not for their protection, but for their destruction! The fact that so many mothers think of their child as a parasite is a scary indictment of our society."[8]

"A woman has a right to control her own body, and no one should tell her what she can or can't do. It's barbaric and unenlightened to force a woman to continue a pregnancy."

In previous chapters, I've addressed the claims that a human embryo is just a "clump of cells," and that a human fetus isn't a person. Some pro-choice advocates still say, "Even if the unborn are human beings, they have fewer rights than the woman. *A woman must have the right to control her own body.*"

One pro-choice advocate, in the face of overwhelming evidence, admitted to me that the unborn are human beings. He then added, "But that's irrelevant to the issue of a woman's right to have an abortion."

But how can someone's humanity be irrelevant to the question of whether someone else has the right to kill him? Wasn't the black person's humanity relevant to the issue of slavery or the Jew's personhood relevant to the ethics of the Holocaust? *Surely the unborn child's humanity and personhood, with the human rights that entails, is the single most relevant issue in the whole abortion debate.*

The "Right to Choose"

While presenting the pro-life position on public school and college campuses, I have sometimes begun by saying, "I'm pro-choice."

Immediately students look relieved, and sometimes even applaud. I then say, "And because I'm pro-choice, I believe every man has the right to rape a woman if that's his choice. After all, it's his body, and we don't have the right to tell him what he can and can't do with it."

In the following seconds, after the shock settles in, I ask them to tell me the fallacy of my argument (which of course I knew well, which is why I am adamantly opposed to what I actually said!). They point out that in asserting the man's right to choose *I ignored the harm done to the innocent woman whose rights have been violated.*

"So are you telling me that you're anti-choice?" I inquire.

After they argue that some choices are wrong and should be illegal, I ask, "So the truth is, you're pro-choice about some choices and anti-choice about other choices, right? And it all depends on what the choice is and whether or not it harms the innocent?"

Yes, they agree. (In that moment pro-choice people are in 100% agreement with pro-life people.)

I respond, "So you're saying that if I can demonstrate to you that a woman's choice to have an abortion harms or kills another human being, then you'll no longer be pro-choice about abortion?"

My hope is that students will heed their own

common sense and their perfectly sound logic—which, somehow, they were failing to apply to the unborn and to abortion.

It's absurd to defend a specific choice simply on the basis that it's a choice. *Every single good or evil thing that has ever been done by one person to another was part of a choice.* The fact that something is a choice tells us absolutely *nothing* about whether or not it's right or should be legal.

Laws That Necessarily Limit Choice

Despite the fact that he's choosing to do what he wants with his own body, a man isn't legally permitted to expose himself. There are laws against public urination, drug use, prostitution, trespassing, and even loitering, even though every one of them involves a choice to do something with one's own body. Most of us agree with these laws, even though they restrict personal freedoms, because they protect the rights and interests of others whose personal freedoms they directly or indirectly violate.

My hand is part of my body, but I'm not free to use it to hit you or steal from you or hurt your child—or mine. *Aren't you glad the law stands against me doing whatever I might want with my own body?*

All of us are in favor of free choice, without the restriction of laws, when it comes to issues like where people choose to live, what kind of car they drive, and a thousand other matters of personal preference that harm no one else. We're also pro-choice in matters of religion, politics, and lifestyle, even when people choose beliefs and behaviors we

31

don't agree with and which we believe bring them harm.

But most of us are decidedly *not* pro-choice when it comes to murder, rape, kidnapping, armed robbery, and child abuse. We know these things aren't discretionary choices that bring harm only to oneself, but bring incalculable harm to *others*. Shouldn't we all recognize that any law that prohibits the victimization of an innocent person is by nature a just law?

But What About a Woman's Rights and Choices?

Of course, any two people are equal and have equal rights. Hence, *a mother has the right to live every bit as much as a child*. I can't emphasize enough that the mother's rights are truly important, and society should protect them. But here is what pro-choice advocates routinely fail to recognize: in the vast majority of abortions, the woman's right to live is *not* an issue, because her life is not in danger. (I'll later take a closer look at the hard cases where the mother's life truly *is* endangered.)

Except in the rare case of pregnancy by rape (I'll also address abortion in cases of rape or incest in a subsequent chapter), a woman carrying a child has made choices of control over her body that resulted in pregnancy. Women are free to choose to abstain from sex or to use birth control or to do neither. But when a woman is pregnant, the choices she has made have produced a new human being. As one woman points out, "After a woman is pregnant, she cannot choose whether or not she wishes to become a mother. She already is, and since the child is already present in her womb, all that is left to her to decide is whether she will deliver her baby dead or alive."[1]

Undoubtedly, an unplanned pregnancy can be difficult, and a woman facing one needs compassion and support, not condemnation. But once the baby is born, the woman is again free to choose: she can raise the child or choose to place him in a loving adoptive home with one of the two million families waiting to adopt.[2]

When a woman chooses to have sex or to use birth control, those two choices are personal and private. But abortion is not personal and private. It directly involves the life of another person and therefore becomes the concern of a decent society. Just as society would protect the life of the mother if someone tried to kill her, so it should protect the life of the child if someone tries to kill her.

"Forcing" a woman to continue a pregnancy, which is a natural function of her body, is not barbaric or primitive, nor is it about pro-life men exerting control over women's bodies, as some claim. It's simply protecting the life of a woman's unborn child, even if she feels her pregnancy is a burden. And given that abortion harms women both physically and mentally, it's protecting her, too, though she may not immediately see it as such. In time, she will likely come to understand that her temporary burden was well worth it to know that her child was rescued from death, and now has a life to live.

What's *truly* barbaric and primitive is unnaturally ending the life of a helpless baby in her mother's womb, which should be the safest place for a child.

It's true that carrying a child is a natural condition that comes with inconvenience. But few women are bedridden during their pregnancies. Most are socially active, capable of working, traveling, and exercising almost to the day the child is delivered. Isn't it reasonable for society to expect an adult to live temporarily with an inconvenience *if the only alternative is killing a child*? Regardless of the challenges, one person's right to a lifestyle, or even bodily autonomy, is not greater than another person's right to live.

Even when pregnancy is unwanted or difficult, it's temporary. Since the vast majority of abortions take place from six weeks to six months of development, the actual difference between the woman who aborts her child and the woman who doesn't is not nine months but three to seven months. In contrast, while pregnancy is a temporary condition, abortion produces a permanent condition—the irreversible death of a human being.

More Than One Body Involved

Pro-choice advocates argue, "Every woman has the right to choose what she does with her own body." Ironically, the choice of abortion assures that something like 431,000 females in the United States each year *don't* have the right to choose what they do with *their* bodies. (That's roughly the number of girls aborted every year in America—approximately half of all aborted children.)

Philosopher Mortimer Adler claimed, as have many others, that the unborn is "a part of the mother's body, in the same sense that an individual's arm or leg is a part of a living organism. An individual's decision to have an arm or leg amputated falls within the sphere of privacy—the freedom to do as one pleases in all matters that do not injure others or the public welfare."[3]

While Adler was a brilliant man, he was apparently ignorant of the biological facts. A body part is defined by the common genetic code it shares with the rest of its body. Inarguably, the unborn child's genetic code differs from his mother's. Every cell of the mother's tonsils, appendix, heart, and lungs shares the same genetic code. *Each and every cell of the unborn child's body belongs uniquely to him and is different than every cell of his mother's body.*

A Chinese zygote (a new human in the earliest stage of development) implanted in a Swedish woman will always be Chinese, not Swedish. Why? Because his biological identity is based on his genetic code, not that of the body in which he resides. If the woman's body were the only one involved in a pregnancy, then it would mean she has two noses, four legs, two sets of fingerprints, two brains, two circulatory systems, and two skeletal systems. Half the time she must also have testicles and a penis. (Can anyone seriously argue that a male child's reproductive organs are part of his mother's body, just because he resides there?)

This is not pro-life rhetoric. Rather, it's an indisputable scientific fact that the mother is one distinctive and self-contained person, and her child is another.

Human Rights for All

A Portland, Oregon abortionist said, "Not everybody is meant to be born. I believe, for a baby, life begins when his mother wants him."[4]

So a human life becomes real only when and if another person values it?

Pro-choice author Barbara Ehrenreich wrote in the *New York Times*, "A woman may think of her fetus as a person or as just cells depending on whether the pregnancy is wanted or not. This does not reflect moral confusion, but choice in action."[5]

According to this Alice-in-Wonderland approach, a mother's choice is the only important reality, overshadowing all matters of indisputable scientific *fact*. If society operated this way, every killing of every person would be justifiable, wouldn't it? The real issue wouldn't be the worth of the person killed, but the free choice of the one doing the killing. If a man doesn't want his wife, he can think of her as a nonperson—indeed many men have done that very thing. If he chooses to kill her, using Ehrenreich's same logic, then it would not be "moral confusion," but "choice in action."

Ms. Ehrenreich goes on to write, "Moreover, a woman may think of the fetus as a person and still find it necessary and morally responsible to have an abortion."[6]

We must not miss the implications of this viewpoint. It says that one may acknowledge the personhood of a fellow human being, yet feel that for one's personal benefit or exercise of choice it is none-theless legitimate—even "morally responsible"—to kill that other person.

Though this is a logical conclusion of abortion-rights thinking, *carrying it out in our society would ultimately mean the end of all human rights and social justice.* Isn't that too high a price to pay for unrestricted freedom of choice?

"It's necessary to be pro-choice in order to protect women's rights. Those, especially men, who push their pro-life convictions on others are anti-women."

When it comes to gender equality and the empowerment of women, there's much that both pro-choice and pro-life people can agree on. Girls and women should be given equal opportunities for education and employment, and legal rights, like the right to vote and run for office. Women should be able to live full lives free of enslavement, abuse, violence, oppression, and discrimination of any kind.

But sadly, the term "women's rights" has been hijacked to not just include access to abortion but often exclusively focus on it. NARAL (National Abortion Rights Action League) says, "When the right to abortion is endangered, the fundamental equality of women is threatened. A woman can never be equal if she is denied the basic right to make decisions for herself and her family."[1]

But is abortion truly necessary to ensure

women's rights, and at the core of what it means to be pro-woman?

The Early Feminists

It might come as a surprise to some that early women's rights advocates were pro-life, not pro-abortion. Susan B. Anthony was a radical feminist in her day. Her newspaper, *The Revolution,* made this claim: "When a woman destroys the life of her unborn child, it is a sign that, by education or circumstances, she has been greatly wronged."

Another pioneer feminist, Elizabeth Cady Stanton, commented on abortion this way: "When we consider that women are treated as property, it is degrading to women that we should treat our children as property to be disposed of as we wish."

The early feminists were followed by a new breed of feminists, such as Margaret Sanger, founder of Planned Parenthood, who advocated abortion as a means of sexual freedom, birth control, and eugenics. (See the appendix.) Sanger, and others who followed her, tied the abortion agenda to the legitimate issues of women's rights. The same thing happened in the sixties. Dr. Bernard Nathanson admitted that he and his fellow abortion-rights strategists deliberately linked the abortion issue to the women's issue so it could be furthered not on its own merits, but on the merits of women's rights.[2]

Early feminists such as Susan Anthony would have been appalled and angered to think that abortion—which they deplored as the killing of innocent children—would one day be linked in people's minds with the cause of women's rights! Alice Paul drafted the original version of the Equal Rights Amendment. She called abortion "the ultimate exploitation of women." There are feminists today who still uphold the pro-life position. Feminists for Life is an active group started in the early 1970s.

Both women and men should be free to affirm certain platforms of the feminist movement without affirming others. One may support some or most feminist ideals, such as equal pay for equal work and no gender-based harassment or glass ceilings, while wholeheartedly opposing abortion because it kills children and therefore ultimately hurts their mothers. In fact, due to the use of amniocentesis for sex selection, and gender prejudice, a disproportionate number of children who are killed worldwide in abortion are females.

A Genocide of the World's Youngest Women

The irony of endorsing the single greatest means of robbing women of their most basic right—the right to life—seems lost on pro-choice feminists. More than half of aborted children are female, and in some cultures prenatal testing is done to identify females and kill them before they are born. This is anti-woman on the most basic level.

In countries such as China and India, there is immense pressure on women to provide male offspring. One Indian woman says, "The taunts from society and from my in-laws that I would have faced for not having a son forced me to abort."[3]

The United Nations Population Fund reports:

Today, around 126 million women are believed to be "missing" around the world—the result of son preference and gender-biased sex selection, a form of discrimination. Since the 1990s, some areas have seen up to 25 per cent more male births than female births. The rise in sex selection is alarming as it reflects the persistent low status of women and girls. The resulting gender imbalance also has a damaging effect on societies. Instances of increased sexual violence and trafficking have already been linked to the phenomenon.[4]

Sex-selective abortions also happen in western countries. The Charlotte Lozier Institute explains, "Current research shows that just a generation ago, sex ratios at birth within certain ethnic communities (specifically 'Asian-Pacific') in the U.S. and UK were within the normal range. Within the last twenty years, the ratio has climbed sharply, resulting in highly unbalanced ratios in favor of males. Such a noticeable change in recent decades implicates the increased use of sex selective abortion."[5]

As the husband of a wonderful woman and the father of two precious grown women, I cannot understand why anyone would not want to have a daughter. But for reasons that reflect some irrational bias against women, females are being targeted for extinction. And the tool for this destruction of women is staunchly defended by those who call themselves pro-woman.

Mental and Physical Effects on Women

The #ShoutYourAbortion campaign has encouraged women to share their stories on social media and "normalize" abortion. But the fact that some women feel their abortion was a good choice doesn't change the fundamental reality that abortion kills children. And it's well documented that abortion *does* harm many women, both physically and mentally. For every woman who "shouts her abortion," there are many more suffering in silence.

In contrast to the claims that abortion is a constructive and liberating alternative, one of the early presidents and spokespersons for Feminists for Life, Frederica Mathewes-Green wrote, "No woman wants an abortion like she wants an ice cream cone or a Porsche. She wants an abortion like an animal caught in a trap wants to gnaw off its own leg."[6]

Women's Health after Abortion is an encyclopedic work citing more than five hundred medical journal articles, demonstrating the adverse effects of abortion on women. The deVeber Institute for Bioethics and Social Research, which produces the book, says, "Some of the consequences of abortion do not surface until long after the procedure, or, as in the case of infertility, remain undetected until the woman wishes to bear a child. Yet at present many studies rely on short-term findings; furthermore, researchers often minimize the significance of their findings, and sometimes even arrive at conclusions that flatly contradict their data."[7]

Dr. Patricia Coleman, professor of Human Development and Family Studies at Bowling Green State University, analyzed outcomes of twenty-two scholarly research papers on women, mental health, and abortion. The research involved well over 877,000 women. She states, "81 percent of females who had an abortion were found to be at an increased risk for mental health problems, including depression, alcohol abuse, and suicidal behaviors."[8] Very similar conclusions to Coleman's were reached independently in an Australian analysis of abortion and mental health data.[9]

Post-abortive women experience physical complications, too.

In her testimony before a Senate subcommittee in 2004, gynecologist and scientist Elizabeth Shadigian testified that "abortion increases rates of breast cancer,[10] placenta previa, preterm births, and maternal suicide. . . . Statistically, all types of deaths are higher with women who have had induced abortions."[11]

Pelvic Inflammatory Disease (PID) is an infection that leads to fever and infertility. Researchers state, "Pelvic infection is a common and serious complication of induced abortion and has been reported in up to 30 percent of all cases." A study of women having first-trimester abortions established that "women with post-abortal pelvic inflammatory disease had significantly higher rates of . . . spontaneous abortion, secondary infertility, dyspareunia [painful intercourse], and chronic pelvic pain."[12]

Women with one abortion double their risk of

cervical cancer, compared to non-abortive women, while women with two or more abortions multiply their risk by nearly five times. Similar elevated risks of ovarian and liver cancer have also been linked to single and multiple abortions.[13]

After extensive investigation, Dr. Joel Brind, a cancer researcher and professor of endocrinology, concluded that there is "a remarkably consistent, significant positive association between induced abortion and breast cancer incidence…"[14] A woman who has an abortion increases her risk of breast cancer by a minimum of 50 percent and as much as 300 percent.[15]

The deVeber Institute for Bioethics and Social Research explains, "Since 2003 five studies have been published showing no link between abortion and breast cancer. However, these studies are either underpowered or use a control group with the same risk characteristics as the women who have had induced abortions."[16]

Many pro-choice organizations and research foundations, such as The National Cancer Institute, reject the idea of any connection between abortion and breast cancer.[17] Unfortunately, like many other organizations, they have vested interests in denying abortion's risks and how it harms women.

Furthermore, the abortion industry's role in empowering the abuse of women trapped in the sex-trafficking industry is often overlooked. One study of 66 human-trafficking survivors found that between them they had 114 abortions, with coercion playing a role in at least some of their abortions. "Notably, the phenomenon of forced abortion as it occurs in sex trafficking transcends the political boundaries of the abortion debate, violating both the pro-life belief that abortion takes innocent life and the pro-choice ideal of women's freedom to make their own reproductive choices."[18] Several investigations have also shown Planned Parenthood's failure to report statutory rape and sexual abuse. One victim said she was taken to Planned Parenthood "because they didn't ask any questions."[19] This is decidedly not pro-woman.

Men, Abortion, and Being Pro-Woman

Pro-choice advocates often say that pro-life men are anti-woman, and the pro-life movement is a way for men to deny women's rights and control their bodies. One pro-choice writer says, "American anti-abortion policy has always been about controlling (white) women and pushing them into their 'proper' place: being subservient and making more babies."[20]

How ironic. Abortion allows and even *encourages* men to sexually exploit women. If the woman does get pregnant, the man can hand over a few hundred dollars and buy a dead child. (He may feel almost heroic for doing so.) When the man is long gone, with no child to support, the woman is left with the burden of having killed her child. "Abortion rights" bring out not the best, but the worst abusive and controlling behavior in men.

Pro-life men are also told by some pro-choice advocates, "No uterus, no opinion" and "No womb, no say." But abortion is a human issue, not a gender issue. Facts, logic, reason, and compassion have no anatomy. Whether they are espoused by men or women is no more relevant than whether they are espoused by black or white people. The point is not the gender of those advancing arguments, but whether or not the arguments are accurate. To believe otherwise is simply sexism.

If men are disqualified from the abortion issue, they should be disqualified on both sides. The vast majority of doctors who perform abortions are men, as are most pro-choice members of congress. Why do pro-choice advocates embrace the judgment of the all-male Supreme Court that legalized abortion in 1973? And why do pro-choice groups donate sizable campaign funds to male legislators who endorse abortion? If men should be eliminated from the abortion debate, shouldn't they be eliminated from both sides?

Both men and women can care deeply about women receiving equal opportunities, rights, and protections, yet oppose abortion because it harms children (of whom half are female) *and* women.

Finally, if pro-life men's motives are suspect as self-serving, then pro-choice men's motives should also be suspect. I sometimes wonder this when I see prominent males who are pro-choice spokesmen: have some of them congratulated themselves for being women's advocates while paying for the abortions of multiple women for whom they are now free to give no emotional support in their darkest hours?

"Opposition to abortion is just a religious opinion."

People often assume that the pro-life position is only based on religious convictions held by those more derisively known as "Bible thumpers."

Like many other pro-life people, my faith in God and in His Word informs my worldview. Believing God created humans in His image leads me to affirm the sanctity of human life. But you don't need to be a Christian, or even align with any religion, to believe that unborn children deserve life.

That's because the abortion issue is really a human life issue—a civil rights issue for the preborn. It's not simply a religious issue, any more than the rights of Jews and African Americans are simply religious issues.

Secular Pro-Lifers

One of my favorite pro-life advocates of all time was Nat Hentoff (1925-2017), the creator and editor of New York's ultraliberal *Village Voice*. He was a self-described "atheist, a lifelong leftist, and a card-carrying member of the ACLU."[1] He detested most of the policies of conservative administrations, and certainly no one could write him off as an evangelical, a Sunday School teacher, or a political conservative. He was the opposite of all these. But he was also an outspoken civil liberties advocate who took constant heat from his liberal colleagues for publicly calling abortion the killing of children.[2] Hentoff wrote, "Being without theology isn't the slightest hindrance to being pro-life."[3]

Though they're certainly outnumbered by religiously-affiliated pro-life organizations, there are groups such as Secular Pro-Life, Atheists Against Abortion, and Pro-Life Humanists. I attended a pro-life rally in Portland while standing beside those holding "Atheists for Life" signs. We had some great conversations!

Pro-Life Humanists describe their stance this way: "We oppose discrimination against biological humans on the grounds of what they look like and how they function, and we believe that abortion should be rejected on the same ground as racism, sexism and ableism—which place greater importance on what the human entity does and looks like, than on what the entity in question actually is."[4]

Kristine Kruszelnicki, the president of Pro-Life Humanists, writes, "I'm an atheist and I'm pro-life because some choices are wrong, violent, and unjust—and I want to do whatever I can to make abortion both unthinkable and unnecessary."[5]

It's noteworthy that though most governments have long been secular, there's hardly a nation in the world where abortion was legal prior to World War II. This shows that while they may be helpful, religious convictions aren't necessary to believe unborn children's lives are worth protecting. Decent societies have always believed that.

What the Polls Say

Many nonreligious people believe that abortion kills children and that it's wrong. Numerous polls show that an anti-abortion position, at least to a certain extent, is held by a majority of citizens (even though when asked to label their position, they may say they're "pro-choice").

A 2015 survey found that regardless of whether they thought abortion should be legal or not, six in ten Americans agreed that abortion is morally wrong. The surveyors noted that "Most Americans, 84%, agree there should be significant restrictions and safe guards associated with the procedure including limits to within the first three months of pregnancy, allowed only in cases of rape, incest, or to save the life of the mother, or never permitted." Only 9% of those surveyed felt that abortion should be available to a woman during all nine months of pregnancy.[6]

Pro-Life Because of the Evidence

For twenty-seven years, Dr. Landrum Shettles was attending obstetrician-gynecologist at Columbia-Presbyterian Medical Center in New York. Shettles was a pioneer in sperm biology, fertility, and sterility. He is internationally famous for being the discoverer of male- and female-producing sperm. His intrauterine photographs of preborn children have appeared in many medical textbooks. Dr. Shettles states:

I oppose abortion. I do so, first, because I accept what is biologically manifest—*that human life commences at the time of conception*—and, second, because I believe it is wrong to take innocent human life under any circumstances. My position is scientific, pragmatic, and humanitarian.[7]

Dr. Bernard Nathanson, an internationally known obstetrician and gynecologist, owned and operated what was at the time the largest abortion clinic in the western hemisphere, and was directly involved in over sixty thousand abortions.

Dr. Nathanson's study of developments in the science of fetology and his use of ultrasound to observe the unborn child in the womb led him to the conclusion that he had made a horrible mistake. Resigning from his lucrative position, Nathanson wrote in the *New England Journal of Medicine* that he was deeply troubled by his "increasing certainty that I had in fact presided over 60,000 deaths."[8]

In his film *The Silent Scream,* Nathanson later stated, "Modern technologies have convinced us that *beyond question the unborn child is simply another human being,* another member of the human community, indistinguishable in every way from any of us." Dr. Nathanson wrote *Aborting America* to inform the public of the realities behind the abortion rights movement of which he had been a primary leader. At the time Dr. Nathanson was an atheist. His conclusions were not even remotely religious, but squarely based on the biological facts.

Nathanson wrote:

I think that abortion policy ought not be beholden to a sectarian creed, but that obviously the law can and does encompass moral convictions shared by a variety of religious interests. In the case of abortion, however, we can and must decide on the biological evidence and on fundamental humanitarian grounds without resorting to scriptures, revelations, creeds, hierarchical decrees, or belief in God. Even if God does not exist, the fetus does.[9]

"We need abortion in cases of rape or incest, or risk to the mother's life."

Pro-choice advocates often focus on rape because of its well-deserved sympathy factor. Their frequent references to this heartbreaking situation leave the false impression that pregnancy due to rape is common, when in truth it is rare.

The most recent data available from the Guttmacher Institute comes from their survey of over 1,200 women, which found that 1.5 percent of abortions reported resulted from rape or incest.[1] There is wide disagreement on the number of pregnancies caused by rape, since neither the U.S. Centers for Disease Control and Prevention nor the U.S. Department of Justice keep data on it.[2]

Whatever the numbers, rape is a horrible crime and women who are victimized by it deserve our sympathy and our help. And in the case of a resulting pregnancy, both victims—mother and child—deserve the best possible care.

Punish the Guilty, Not the Innocent

Rape is so horrible that when a pregnancy results, we easily transfer our horror to the wrong object. Yet we must not let the ugliness of rape or incest reflect upon either the innocent woman or the innocent child (who is not a stain to be blotted out or a cancer to be removed, but a living human being). Certainly, we must punish the rapist. But let's not punish the innocent child in our rage against the perpetrator.

Rape is never the fault of the child. If you found out today that your biological father had raped your mother, would you feel you no longer had a right to live? Should you go to jail for your father's crimes? Likewise, why should Person A be killed because Person B raped Person A's mother?

A Parallel of Violence

There's a close parallel between the violent attack on a woman in a rape and the violent attack on a child in an abortion. Both are done at the expense of an innocent person. The violence of abortion is never a solution to the violence of rape.

Imposing capital punishment on the innocent child of a sex offender does nothing bad to the rapist and nothing good for the mother. Creating a second victim doesn't undo the damage to the first.

One feminist group says, "Some women have reported suffering from the trauma of abortion long after the rape trauma has faded."[3] It is hard to imagine a worse therapy for a woman who has been raped than to add the guilt and turmoil of having her child killed. What she truly needs is compassionate support, help, and counseling.

A Child Is a Child

A child conceived by rape is as precious as a child conceived by love, because a child is a child. The point is not *how* he was conceived but *that* he was conceived. What if you found that your spouse or adopted child or close friend was fathered by a rapist? Would it change your view of their worth? Would you love them any less? If not, why should we view the innocent unborn child any differently?

I'll never forget speaking to a group and saying every child, regardless of the circumstances of their conception, deserves to live. Afterward a young woman came up to me weeping and was finally able to say, "I've always heard abortion is right when pregnancy is the result of rape, but that's how I was conceived. And this was the first time I've ever heard someone say I deserved to live! My mother was raped when she was twelve. She gave birth to me and gave me up for adoption to a wonderful family. I'll probably never meet her, but every day I thank God for her and her parents. If they hadn't let me live, I wouldn't be here to have my own husband and children and my own life."

There are many who have publicly shared their stories about finding out they were conceived through rape, and are grateful for the life they've been given. Ryan Bomberger, whose biological mother was raped, writes:

As an adoptee who grew up *wanted and loved* in a multiracial family of fifteen and as a happily married adoptive father with four children, I'm here to say there's another side of this painful issue. There are others like me who were conceived in the violence of rape, like my friend Rebecca Kiessling, an attorney and passionate defender of life. There's the former Miss Pennsylvania, Valerie Gatto, Trayvon Clifton, Monica Kelsey, Jim Sable, Pam Stenzel, and many more whose stories offer a different perspective than mainstream media's myopic pro-abortion view. There are women who became mothers from rape who courageously chose life, like Jennifer Christie, Liz Carl, and Rebekah Berg.

…When it comes to rape and abortion, how do you heal violence with more violence?[4]

I have a good friend who was raped and became pregnant. She decided to give birth to the baby and place her for adoption. It was very difficult, but she knows she made the right decision and when she sees pictures of her daughter she overflows with thanksgiving. Her joy is in stark contrast to our friends who remember their abortions and are sometimes overwhelmed by feelings of emptiness and regret. (These women need to hear the message of complete forgiveness by the grace of Jesus![5])

Children Conceived in Incest

Incest is a horrible crime. Offenders should be punished, and victims should be carefully protected from further abuse. The abuser—not the mother or her child—is the problem. Intervention, protection, and ongoing personal help for the mother—and child—are the solution.

Despite popular beliefs, fetal deformity is rare in such cases, and even so, a disabled child still deserves to live. All that's true of children conceived in rape is true of those conceived in incest.

Women often think that a child conceived by such a vile act as rape or incest will be a constant reminder of their pain. On the contrary, the innocence of the child often has a healing effect. The woman can also give another family an incredible gift by allowing them to adopt her child.

After reading an article I'd written about this subject, a woman wrote this to our ministry:

> Many friends thought they were being supportive by bombarding me with their opinions about what to do. I love them dearly, but they weren't helping. As I took my time with this I found myself becoming excited at the fact of having a baby come from such an act of violence. I anticipated issues where the father was concerned but he never came around again. My son is the best addition to my life I could've ever wished for and I consider myself blessed in every way, and my friends and I learned what support means and how to better be there for each other.

What About Abortion When a Woman's Life Is at Risk?

While he was U. S. Surgeon General, Dr. C. Everett Koop stated that in his thirty-eight years as a pediatric surgeon, he never faced a single situation in which an unborn child's life had to be taken in order to save the life of the mother.

In an ectopic pregnancy, the child developing outside the uterus has no hope of survival, and may have to be removed to save his mother's life. A tragic situation, to be sure, but even if one life must be lost, the life that can be saved should be. More often than not, that life is the mother's, not the child's. There are rare cases in later stages of pregnancy when the mother can't be saved, but the baby can be, through delivery. Again, one life saved is better than two lives lost.

Dr. John Crown, an oncologist who has treated pregnant cancer patients, told his Twitter followers he's never had a case where abortion was necessary to save the mother's life.[6] He writes,

> What I say to most patients is, "I know this sounds like the worst thing that could happen but there is a high chance you are going to get two happy outcomes here: you will be cured and the baby will be born normal. That is the most likely outcome. . . ."[7]

A Woman's Life, or Health?

The mother's *life* and *health* are usually two distinct considerations. A pregnant woman with toxemia will have adverse health reactions and considerable inconvenience. Though difficult, this isn't normally a threat to her life.

Once a baby reaches the third trimester, if a

woman's life is threatened, the child can be delivered and, in many cases, has good odds for survival. Dr. Omar L. Hamada, a board-certified OB/GYN who has delivered over 2,500 babies, wrote, "I want to clear something up so that there is absolutely no doubt. …There's not a single fetal or maternal condition that requires third trimester abortion. Not one. Delivery, yes. Abortion, no."[8]

Sometimes pregnancy itself—because of routine medical appointments and tests—can actually serve as a catalyst for discovering an otherwise undetected illness. But serious illnesses that may rarely occur during a pregnancy can still be treated to protect the mother and her baby. Breast cancer is identified in about one out of every three thousand pregnancies and is usually entirely treatable.[9]

Consistently Pro-Life

Friends of ours were faced with a fast-spreading uterine cancer in which removing the cancer would result in the unborn child's death. They knew that to wait for the child to become viable meant both mother and child would die from the cancer. It was heartbreaking, but they and we were confident that the decision to save the mother's life was right.

However, this was not an abortion. The purpose of the surgery was not to kill the child, but to save the life of the mother, and was therefore a consistently pro-life act. The child's death was a tragic, unintended consequence of life-saving efforts. Being pro-life isn't just about babies—being pro-life is also about women, who are every bit as valuable as babies.

In the very rare case when a choice has to be made between the baby's life or that of the mother, it's up to the mother and father to decide together. There have been cases where a mother has refused life-saving treatment in order to continue her pregnancy and give her child life. But no one should fault those who act to save the life of the mother when it appears both lives can't be saved.

Abortion to save the mother's life (before a baby could be safely delivered and survive) was legal before convenience abortion was legalized and would continue to be legal if abortion were made illegal again. Claims of pro-choice advocates to the contrary, there's no danger whatsoever that women whose lives are in jeopardy would be unable to get treatment, even if such treatment tragically results in the death of their unborn child.

"Every child should be a wanted child."

Planned Parenthood has argued that unwanted children "get lower grades, particularly in language skills." In the past they've said that unwanted adolescents "perform increasingly poorly in school," And "they are less than half as likely as wanted children to pursue higher education."[1] Many people have also expressed concern that having more unwanted children results in more child abuse.

I don't question the accuracy of these findings, or the concerns presented about at-risk children. They tell us what we should already know—the importance of wanting and caring for our children. Instead, however, pro-choice advocates use such research to justify getting rid of "unwanted" children by aborting them!

Furthermore, how would we know if many of those abused children were actually "wanted" children at birth but later became "unwanted" because of the selfishness of the parents? We can't automatically connect an abused child with an "unwanted" pregnancy.

Let's be clear: everyone, pro-lifers and pro-choicers alike, agrees that children should be wanted, cherished, and loved. However, the word *unwanted* shouldn't be used to describe a child but rather, an attitude of some adults toward the child. *The real problem isn't unwanted children, but unwanting adults.*

No Unwanted Child

There are "unwanted" pregnancies, but in reality *there is no such thing as an unwanted child.* While certain people may not want them, other people do, desperately. By some estimates, there are 2 million American couples waiting to adopt. This means "there are as many as 36 waiting families for every one child who is placed for adoption."[2] Newborns are especially desired. It's important to clarify that this has no direct bearing on the moral issue of abortion. Even if no one wanted to adopt a baby, it would still not be right to kill her. The point is simply that *every child is wanted by someone.*

Feelings Change

Many children who are at first unwanted by their mothers are very much wanted later in the pregnancy and even more at birth. (Unfortunately, many women who would have wanted the child by their fifth month of pregnancy, when they are delighted to feel her kick, get an abortion in their third month.)

Furthermore, many children wanted at birth are *not* wanted when they are crying at 2 a.m. six weeks later. Should whether or not the parents want the baby still determine whether she deserves to live? If that's a legitimate standard before birth, why not after?

Addressing the issue of unwanted children, Abort73 says:

> [Abortion advocates] don't argue that mothers should be free to kill their "unwanted" children *after* birth because they know these children are living, human beings with full rights of personhood. The only reason they argue that mothers should be free to kill their unwanted children *before* birth is because they're ignoring the scientific reality that these children, too, are living, human beings. The question is humanity, not wantedness.[3]

"Wanting" is simply one person's subjective and changeable feeling toward another. The "unwanted" wife or girlfriend is a real person deserving to be treated with dignity and love, and worthy of being protected rather than abused. The fact that her husband or boyfriend feels differently doesn't make her less of a person. Likewise, the "unwanted" child is a real person regardless of anyone else's feelings toward her. Certainly she doesn't deserve brutal abuse by abortion.

Whose Best Interests?

One day my wife was calmly sharing with a pro-choice woman why she is pro-life. The woman looked at Nanci and said, "Haven't you seen the homeless kids on the streets of our city? It's *cruel* for them to have to live in a world like this!" My wife said, "OK, why don't you and I get some guns and go kill those children right now? Let's put them out of their misery." The woman was shocked (I was a little stunned myself), but Nanci made her point. Let's not pretend it's an act of love to kill people just because they're unwanted!

One of the most ironic and misleading aspects of the pro-choice argument is making it appear that abortion is in the best interests of the child. This is so absurd as to be laughable—were it not so tragic. A little person is torn limb from limb, *for her benefit*? (Who are we kidding?)

Today people say, "I can't have this child because I can't give it a good life." And what is their solution to not being able to give him a good life? To take from him the only life he has (while refusing to place him in the hands of those who *long* to give him a good life).

One of the Strangest Pro-Choice Arguments

In 1973, when abortion was legalized, child abuse cases in the United States were estimated at 167,000 annually.[4] In 2017 there were 674,000 substantiated cases of abuse and 1,720 fatalities, over four times the rate of abuse before abortion was legalized.[5]

The pervasive notion that aborting a child prevents child abuse is one of the strangest arguments ever made. It is true in exactly the same sense that this statement is true: *killing one's wife prevents wife abuse.* True, dead people are no longer here to be abused. In that sense, future abuses can be prevented by killing them now. But arguing that we have saved them from abuse by killing them is surely convoluted logic.

We should ask ourselves *why* far more children in America have been abused since abortion was legalized than before. I believe a large part of the answer is that *abortion has changed the way we view children.* The attitude that results in abortion is exactly the same attitude that results in child abuse: children are seen as an inconvenience, and adults imagine they have the right not to be inconvenienced by a child.

If parents believe they had a right to abort but didn't, the mother or father can look at their sick and crying baby in the middle of the night and think, "I could have aborted you," or even, "I *should* have aborted you." The false assumption is the child owes her parents everything; they owe their child nothing. This can cause resentment for any demands or needs of the child that require parental sacrifice. The logic, whether conscious or unconscious, is inescapable. If it was all right—even lauded as courageous or loving by some—to kill the same baby before birth, is it really so bad to slap him around once in a while now?

The solution to battering children outside the womb is not battering children inside the womb. The key to preventing child abuse isn't doing the abuse *earlier.* It's not doing the abuse at all.

For those who are unable or unwilling to raise a child in a healthy environment, there's always the choice of adoption (and as we've seen, there is great demand for adoptable newborns).

A More Honest Slogan

Planned Parenthood's famous slogan used in past decades was this: "Every child a wanted child." As

I used to say in abortion debates, this is something we should all agree with. Where we disagree is in the proper way to finish the sentence. How do *you* think the sentence should be finished?

- *Every child a wanted child*, so . . . let's place children in homes where they're wanted, and let's learn to value and want children more.
- *Every child a wanted child*, so . . . let's identify unwanted children before they're born and kill them by abortion.

Everyone agrees that children should be wanted. The only question is this: Should we get rid of the *unwanting* or get rid of the *children?*

When it comes to the unborn, the abortion rights position is more accurately reflected in a different slogan, one that doesn't look so good on a bumper sticker: "Every unwanted child a dead child."

"Forcing a woman to keep a child she can't afford to raise and who will limit her opportunities in life—or to give up a child for adoption—is cruel."

Despite their emphasis on choice, the pro-choice movement leaves many women feeling that they have no choice but abortion. Abortion is constantly portrayed as the preferred choice. After all, a woman facing an unplanned pregnancy wonders, what's the alternative? Raise a child she seemingly can't afford, and who will disrupt her life choices like going to school and pursuing a career? Or experience the heartbreak of giving up a child for adoption?

But "abortion or misery" is a binary trap that keeps women from pursuing—and society from providing—positive alternatives. It's a terrible thing to present pregnant women with inadequate choices, leaving them in an apparent no-win situation. We must reject this trap of presenting the choice between abortion and misery, as if there were no misery in abortion, and as if there were no alternatives.

Why does Planned Parenthood, with its over one billion dollars from tax revenues and foundations,[1] not devote itself to a third alternative, such as adoption? Since it makes millions of dollars from abortions every year, giving it huge vested interests in abortion, how can Planned Parenthood be expected to offer real and objective choices to pregnant women in need?

Do they share the stories of women who kept their children, and are grateful they did? How about the stories of women who chose adoption, and though it was difficult, have been left with a sense of peace, knowing they have given someone the gift of life? Or how about the wonderful stories of women who have been reunited with their birth children years later?

Does Motherhood Mean Poverty and No Opportunities?

Many women attest that being a mother doesn't ruin their lives, as is sometimes claimed, but expands and enriches them in beautiful ways, even when it's challenging emotionally, physically, and financially. Unfortunately, that possibility is likely the farthest thing from the mind of a woman who finds herself pregnant and wishes she weren't.

Maria Baer, a volunteer counselor at her local pregnancy resource center, writes:

> Women facing an unplanned pregnancy often have reasonable, here-and-now fears. They may fear the loss of financial stability—or the loss of the ability to ever reach it. They may fear the loss of an already teetering status

quo in which every available ounce of food is already consumed at home—perhaps by other children they're already parenting. Pregnant women may lose a job, or they may not get the job they were hoping for. They may fear a violent boyfriend or father.

They may even fear pregnancy itself, which is often full of terrifying sickness, physical pain, loss of emotional control, and embarrassing bodily problems. ...That means one of our first steps in ministering to a woman facing a crisis pregnancy is to acknowledge her fear. Don't judge it, don't shrug it off, but take her seriously. It *is* scary. Don't offhandedly offer adoption as a quick solution. Don't immediately start in on the logical fallacies of pro-abortion apologetics. Let her be afraid, and tell her she's not alone. (Better yet: Mean it.)

Once we acknowledge her fear—and, if she'll allow it, pray for her—we can start to talk through potential solutions to her various worries.[2]

These fears are all understandable. But because the life of another human being is involved, financial distress does not justify abortion. It *does* mean that women who choose to keep and raise their children instead of choosing adoption need support and help. There are pro-life organizations in the U.S., including pregnancy resource centers (which outnumber abortion clinics), Young Lives (a branch of Young Life), Students for Life, and Feminists for Life, that offer support for pregnant and parenting students. "College pro-life groups also have been working to make campuses more friendly, welcoming environments for student-parents by advocating for diaper changing tables in restrooms, offering free babysitting, and encouraging the school to adopt policies to accommodate pregnant/parenting students."[3]

Feminists for Life addresses the situation of a pregnant woman who is poor and lacks support:

> A woman who is pregnant needs to know that there are perfect strangers who will care for her even if the people she counts on the most have let her down. She needs information about child support laws that prohibit coercion by the father either by physical force or by threats to withhold child support.
>
> ...We do not eliminate poverty by eliminating poor women's children. It is degrading to poor women to expect or imply that their children aren't welcome. We believe that poor women deserve the same support and life-affirming alternatives as wealthy women.
>
> ...Abortion is not an enriching experience. An abortion won't get a woman a better job or get her out of a bad (for example, abusive) situation.[4]

Completing school and working are desirable things in many cases, and perhaps even necessary financially. Pregnancy can make them difficult. But a woman normally can continue school and work during pregnancy. If she places her child for adoption, she need not give up school or work. If she chooses to raise the child herself, there are childcare options available if she must work outside the home. Help is available in many forms.

I am not suggesting this is ideal, nor do I say it callously. I have worked with and helped single mothers and know their difficulties. I am simply pointing out there are alternatives, any one of which is preferable to an innocent child's death and the undesirable consequences to her mother. Regardless of the challenges, *one person's right to a preferred lifestyle is not greater than another person's right to a life.*

Furthermore, when the only choice presented is abortion, a woman is frequently kept in a negative cycle which can result in multiple abortions. Having and raising a child or choosing adoption can be an enriching and growing experience in taking responsibility, thereby possibly resulting in better choices in the future.

Is Adoption: a "Regrettable Punishment"?

I am amazed at the negative light in which adoption is often portrayed in abortion rights literature. Pro-choice advocates Carole Anderson and Lee Campbell say of adoption, "The unnecessary separation of mothers and children is a cruel, but regrettably usual, punishment that can last a lifetime."[5]

Adoption is hardly a punishment to a woman carrying a child. It is a heaven-sent alternative to raising a child she is unprepared to raise, or to killing that same child. Adoption is a fine alternative that saves a life and makes another family happy; it's tragic that adoption is so infrequently chosen as an alternative to abortion. (As cited earlier, there are two million families waiting to adopt, and newborns are especially desired by adoptive families.)

Maria Baer writes,

> Women may fear…adoption. Though morally clear, the thought is often experientially vague: It seems, or feels, much less repugnant to have a hidden medical procedure in the first weeks of pregnancy than to consciously hand over a smiling, babbling baby to a woman whose body never knew him or her. It's cognitive dissonance, sure, but it's a real—and understandable—fear.[6]

One way of addressing a woman's fear is to demonstrate the beauty and courage of allowing another family to adopt. Because a woman has not yet bonded with her child, the abortion might seem like an easy solution, while parting with her child after birth might be emotionally difficult. *But the child's life is just as real before bonding as after.*

I've talked with several women considering abortions who had identical reactions to the suggestion of adoption: "What kind of mother would I be to give up a child for adoption?" The better question, which we need to gently help her ask, is, "What kind of mother would I be to kill my baby by abortion?"

The reason the former question is asked more often than the latter is our capacity to deny reality. Pregnant women who think "I don't want to be a mother" tell themselves, under the influence of pro-choice rhetoric, that they still have a choice about becoming a mother. There are certainly choices open to them, including whether or not to raise their child themselves or place their child for adoption. Both choices require sacrificial love, for sure. But the fact is, they have no choice about whether or not they are mothers. That ship sailed the moment they became pregnant—the moment the baby was conceived.

Many years ago we took a pregnant teenage girl into our home. Though she'd had two abortions, she chose to carry this baby and, with our help and support, placed him for adoption. It was not easy, but this wonderful woman (one husband and three more children later) told me: "I look back at the three babies I no longer have, but with very different feelings. The two I aborted fill me with grief and regret. But when I think of the one I gave up for adoption, I'm filled with joy, because I know he's being raised by a wonderful family that wanted him." Several years ago she was able to meet her grown biological son, in a gathering arranged by his adopted mother. My wife, Nanci, and I were invited to attend this reunion. It was one of the most unforgettable and truly wonderful experiences of our lives. We witnessed the beautiful result of a painful but courageous decision made 33 years earlier. *Everyone* present at this reunion, without exception, had great reason to celebrate!

A woman facing an unplanned pregnancy has no easy options. She has three choices—have her child and raise him, have her child and allow another family to raise him, or kill her child through abortion. Two of these options are reasonable and constructive. One is not. I believe it's a moral imperative that we clearly tell pregnant women, "You can choose life and goodness and a future for your child without raising him or her yourself."

Tragically, too often "pro-choice" ends up meaning "no choice but abortion." Let's do all we can to show women the *real* choices besides abortion—which are far superior, with outcomes involving life, not death.

"No one should be made to carry,
deliver, and care for a disabled child
with lifelong needs, nor should
a child be condemned to a lifetime
of suffering."

In her *New York Times* article "I Had a Late-Term Abortion. I Am Not a Monster," one woman shared her story of expecting a little girl with severe brain abnormalities uncovered by prenatal testing. She and her husband were told their daughter would face seizures and cognitive impairment along with other unknown issues, so they decided to end her life through a late-term abortion.

The author writes,

> I regret that we had to make the choice. I regret that she was so sick, so broken. But I do not regret the decision we made. Within 15 minutes of the diagnosis, we knew what we had to do: We would become baby killers.
>
> …When people ask, "How could you?" I reply that allowing her to live would have been a fate worse than death. Her diagnosis was not fatal, not incompatible with the

bare mechanics of a living body. But it was incompatible with a fulfilling life. And that makes all the difference to me. That's why I call myself "pro-life."[1]

Later she says, "I know I made the best choice for my child. I do not regret it and I will not hide it."

Her article represents a chilling shift in our culture's discussion about abortion, especially when the unborn is found to have a disability. To some, it is no longer taboo to admit that a woman is expecting a child, not just a mass of cells. The author candidly refers to her unborn child as her daughter. But because her child had a severe handicap, to her, and to others in our society, abortion is seen as a compassionate choice in the face of disability, even "the best choice."

But is that really the case?

A Cultural Blind Spot

On the one hand, our society provides special parking, ramps, and elevators for the disabled. We talk tenderly about those poster children with spina bifida and Down syndrome. We sponsor the Special Olympics and cheer on the competitors, speaking of the joy and inspiration they bring us. But when we hear a woman is carrying one of these very children, many say, "Kill it."

Here in my home state of Oregon, in 2012, a couple was awarded nearly three million dollars—the amount they claim the extra care for raising their Down syndrome daughter will cost—in what was called a wrongful birth lawsuit. They sued the hospital for negligence after doctors told them prenatal tests showed their child would not have that disability. The hospital's mistake saved the child's life, because the parents claim they would have aborted her had they known.[2] (What message does that send to their child?)

But if a disability should be a license to kill someone, why limit it to the unborn? The same child with the same disability is a great expense and inconvenience at any age, isn't he? Suppose your six-year-old suddenly becomes blind or paraplegic. He's now a burden. Raising him is expensive, inconvenient, and hard on your mental health. If a law were passed that made it legal to put him to death, would you do it? If not, why not?

You wouldn't kill your handicapped child *because you know him.* But killing an unborn child just because you haven't held him in your arms and can't hear his cry doesn't change his nature or his value. Give yourself a chance to know your child. You *will* love him. Laura Nicole writes, "The mindset that preborn babies with disabilities must be aborted is based on a misguided sense of compassion rooted in despair. In a society that values the advancement of treatments for those suffering difficult conditions, medical developments continue to bring new hope to those suffering from serious conditions. Unfortunately, it seems that children in the womb are rarely afforded this new hope granted to those outside the womb."[3]

What about the anencephalic child who doesn't

have a fully developed brain? Since the common expectation is "he will die anyway," doctors often advise parents to have an abortion.[4] But it's one thing to know a child will probably die, and entirely another to choose to take his life.

Many families have had precious experiences naming, holding, and bonding with an anencephalic baby after birth.[5] I personally know such people who are forever grateful they gave their precious child the chance to join their family and be loved every day of his short life. This is in stark contrast to the unhealthy grief and guilt that comes from taking his life. Abortion does not eliminate grief. Indeed, it ultimately magnifies it.

Children Who Need More Love

An often overlooked but indisputable point is that doctors and prenatal tests *can* be wrong. Many parents have aborted their babies because physicians told them their children would be severely handicapped. Others I've talked with were told the same thing but chose to let their babies live. These parents were then amazed to give birth to children without disabilities. (Who knows how many children have been aborted because of a mistaken test or diagnosis?)

However, more often than not, medical tests and doctors' diagnoses are accurate, and the child *is* born with a serious deformity. To be sure, it is hard to raise a disabled child. He requires extra attention and effort. What makes this a hard case, however, is not whether the child deserves to live or die. What is hard is the difficult responsibilities that letting him live will require of his parents.

The film *The Elephant Man* depicts the true story of John Merick. He was a terribly deformed young man, rejected and ridiculed, until someone took the time to know him and discover that he was a wonderful human being. Merick said, "My life is full because I know that I am loved."

Nick Vujicic was born in 1982, in Melbourne, Australia, without arms and legs. He has lived nearly forty years without the ability to walk, care for his most basic needs, or even embrace those he loves. For twenty years, he has been speaking internationally and has also founded an organization called Life Without Limbs. (Nick is married and the father of four children.)

It's fair to say that most children with such disabilities would be aborted. But Nick is one of countless people living meaningful and inspirational lives because they were given the chance and have been raised with sacrificial love. His life has not been easy, and for a time he struggled with thoughts of suicide. But so too have countless people who are not disabled. People are people regardless of the degree of their physical limitations.

A young man born without a left leg and without arms below the elbows says, "When I was born, the first thing my dad said to my mom was that 'this one needs our love more.'"[6] Not only were these parents just what their son needed, he was just what they needed. Many families have drawn together and found joy and strength in having a child with mental or physical handicaps.

If you asked a disabled person if they wish their parents would have aborted them, what response would you expect? If you asked the parents of disabled children if they wish their children had never been born, what would you think they'd say? Who is better qualified than the disabled and their parents to address the issue of whether children should be aborted because of disabilities?

Does this mean caring for a disabled child and seeing her suffering isn't extremely difficult? No, of course not. But hope and beauty in difficult situations are often only seen and appreciated in the rearview mirror.

A Meaningful Life?

Some still argue: "It's cruel to let a handicapped child be born to a meaningless life." We may define a meaningful life one way, but we should ask ourselves what is meaningful to the disabled themselves.

Spina bifida patients were asked whether their handicaps made life meaningless and if they should have been allowed to die after birth. "Their unanimous response was forceful. Of course they wanted to live! In fact, they thought the question was ridiculous."[7]

Handicapped children are often happy, always precious, and usually delighted to be alive. S. E. Smith, in an article in *Disability* says, "The able-bodied, who control much of society, need to break themselves of the beliefs that life with a disability is tragic, not worth living."[8]

In the 1980s, a survey of pediatricians and pediatric surgeons revealed that more than two out of three would go along with parents' wishes to deny lifesaving surgery to a child with Down syndrome. Nearly three out of four said that if they had a Down syndrome child, they would choose to let him starve to death. [9]

Years ago, the television series "Life Goes On" portrayed a teenager named Corky who had Down syndrome. The starring role was played by Chris Burke, a young man with Down syndrome, and people were amazed by his winsome performance. Critics raved. But many of the same critics, being pro-choice, would have fully defended the right to kill Chris/Corky, and children like him, before they were born.

This is not only horrible, but baffling, since many Down children are the happiest you'll ever meet. These children require special care, of course, but surely they deserve to be born and to live as much as any of us.

A 2011 study by Harvard University researchers found that rather than leading lives of suffering, people with Down syndrome have unusually high rates of happiness. An amazing 99 percent said they are happy with their lives, 97 percent like who they are, and 96 percent like how they look. The researchers concluded, "Overall, the overwhelming majority of people with Down syndrome surveyed indicate they live happy and fulfilling lives." [10]

"A slew of recent studies has shown that people with Down syndrome report happier lives than us 'normal' folk. Even happier than rich, good looking and intelligent people." [11]

Wouldn't you suppose we'd want more people of any group characterized by such happiness? Tragically, however, studies show that of mothers who receive a positive diagnosis of Down syndrome during the prenatal period, 89 to 97 percent choose abortion.[12]

This means that the children most likely to be happy are also most likely to be killed before birth. Reports show that Iceland's abortion rate for unborn Down syndrome babies is almost 100%. Denmark's is 98%.[13]

Charlotte Fien is a young British woman who eloquently challenged an UN "expert" on human rights who advocates for aborting Down syndrome babies. She said,

> Mr. Ben Achour, your comments about people with Down syndrome deeply offend me. I felt you attacked me for being who I am. Who am I, Mr. Ben Achour? I'm a human being just like you. Our only difference is an extra chromosome.
>
> My extra chromosome makes me far more tolerant than you, sir. . . . If any other heritable traits like skin color were used to eradicate a group of people, the world would cry out. Why are you not crying out when people like me are being made extinct? What have WE done to make you want us to disappear? As far as I know my community doesn't hate, discriminate, or commit crimes. . . .
>
> I keep hearing you use the word "suffering"

in relation to Down syndrome. The ONLY thing we have to suffer are horrible people who want to make us extinct. I have a brilliant life. I have a family that loves me. I have great friends. I have an active social life.

Mr. Ben Achour, what you are suggesting is eugenics. It's disgusting and evil. You need to apologize for your horrible comments. You should also be removed from the Human Rights Committee as an expert. You are not an expert about Down syndrome. You sir, do not speak for my community. The Human Rights Committee needs people who will genuinely fight for the rights of others who are being oppressed. I suggest that the Human Rights Committee appoint me as an expert. I will fight for our right to exist for the rest of my life.[14]

Eighteen-year-old Natalie Dedreux from Cologne asked German Chancellor Angela Merkel a tough question about Germany's abortion laws:

Mrs. Merkel, you are a politician. You make laws. I'm an editor at a magazine for people like me who have Down syndrome. Nine out of ten babies with Down syndrome in Germany aren't born. A baby with Down syndrome can be aborted days before the birth, in what is called 'late stage abortion.' My colleagues and I want to know what your opinion on late-stage abortion is, Mrs.

Merkel. Why can babies with Down syndrome be aborted shortly before birth?...I don't want to be aborted, I want to be born.[15]

When Frank Stephens, a young man with Down syndrome, gave a speech before a U.S. House appropriations panel, he told members of Congress, "Just so there is no confusion, let me say that I am not a research scientist. However, no one knows more about life with Down syndrome than I do. Whatever you learn today, please remember this: I am a man with Down syndrome and my life is worth living."[16]

Let's not pretend. When adults kill a disabled or disadvantaged child, preborn or born, we aren't doing it for his good, but for what we think is our own. We aren't preventing cruelty to the child; we're committing cruelty to the child in order to prevent perceived difficulty for ourselves.

No Justification

Difficult situations such as the one at the beginning of this chapter can cloud our judgment and blur the line between right and wrong. But no matter how seemingly noble the intentions, ending the life of a disabled unborn child through abortion is *never* the "compassionate" choice.

Abort73 says,

Disability isn't the issue, it's humanity. We do not kill people for their disabilities, period. Therefore, unless we're not human beings before we're born, our disabilities should no more disqualify us from life before birth than they do after birth.

...Suffering and hardship are not bad things. They are means to a greater end, a crucial part of the human journey. Anyone who tries to eliminate suffering by killing the "sufferers" is establishing a horrific trend. It is not for us to decide who has a life worth living and who doesn't, and we certainly wouldn't want someone else making that decision for us![17]

The quality of a society is largely defined by how it treats its weakest members. Killing the innocent is never justified because it relieves others of a burden. It's not a solution to inflict suffering on one person in order to avoid it in another, or to kill one person to supposedly prevent their future suffering. If we abort children because of their handicaps—and make no mistake about it, they *are* children—we jeopardize all handicapped people.

PRO-CHOICE CLAIM #11

"The world is overpopulated, so the fewer births the better."

In the 1960s, there was a widespread fear that the world was swarming with people and we were quickly running out of space. Many people are very concerned about this today. Yet it's been calculated that the entire world population of over 7 billion people could be placed in one gigantic city within the borders of the state of Texas, with a smaller population density than many cities around the world.[1] The rest of the globe would be completely empty of people. (Of course, this doesn't account for the land that would be needed in addition to produce food and resources. It simply demonstrates that the living space occupied by seven billion people is considerably less than we imagine.)

Does this mean there's no overcrowding and that our resources are infinite? Of course not. The world is full of problems, including poverty and starvation. But studies consistently show that enough food is presently produced to feed every person on the planet, including the projected worldwide population of 10 billion by 2050.[2]

The problem of starvation is caused by a combination of many factors, including natural disasters, wars, lack of technology, misuse of resources, waste, greed, government indifference or inefficiency, and failure to distribute food properly. None of these has a direct cause and effect link to overpopulation. It is simplistic and inaccurate to attribute most of our global problems to overpopulation.

U.S. Birthrate Below Replacement Level

Consider the current birthrate in America, which is less than what is needed to maintain our population level. In 1957 the average American woman in her reproductive years bore 3.7 children. Considering all causes of death and the increases in average life span, zero population growth requires that the average woman bear 2.1 children.

The fertility rate first fell below replacement levels in 1972. Since then, there have only been two years where the fertility rate has reached at least 2.1 children.[3] That means for several decades, we've been below zero population growth. The sociological perils we face are not those of population explosion, but population reduction.

According to the U.S. Census Bureau, every 18 seconds, the U.S. population grows by about one person[4] as a result of the more than 1 million immigrants who arrive in the U.S. each year.[5] Also, people are living longer than ever before.

In an article on the issue of abortion and overpopulation, Abort73 says:

> While birth rates have decreased, immigration and life expectancy have increased. Of

the three factors that influence population growth, the number of babies being born is by far the least significant. And yet, does anyone suggest that killing immigrants or killing those over 65 is a reasonable way to limit population growth? No. So why would anyone suggest that killing unborn humans is a reasonable way to limit population growth?[6]

The Threat of a Declining Population

Population decrease isn't only an issue for the United States. It is a serious threat to the social and economic prosperity of many countries. Most western European countries are now experiencing economic problems that their governments attribute to population reduction. Several countries around the world, including Germany, Singapore, Japan, and Russia, have even offered prospective parents incentives for having a baby.[7] Why would a government pay its people to have children? Because it recognizes that all societies need a continuous influx of the young in order to remain healthy.

Steven W. Mosher, President of the Population Research Institute, says:

Contrary to what you might hear, the most pressing problem in country after country today is not overpopulation, but underpopulation. In a time of fiscal austerity, the last thing that we need to be doing is spending more tax dollars to drive down the birth rate, reducing the amount of human capital available, and making us all poorer in the long run.[8]

The problem of a shrinking population propagates itself. Because today's women have fewer children, there will be fewer parents tomorrow, resulting in still fewer children. Fewer and fewer people having fewer and fewer children adds up to dying societies.

Legalized abortion has resulted in over 60 million fewer taxpayers in America to support the elderly. An article for the National Public Radio explains that "In many countries, including the U.S., workers pay for retirees' pensions. Fewer kids mean fewer workers funding those pensions."[9]

The future of Social Security is in peril because there are fewer workers to support it:

The Social Security program matured in the 1960s, when Americans were consistently having fewer children, living longer, and earning wages at a slower rate than the rate of growth in the number of retirees. As these trends have continued, today there are just 2.9 workers per retiree—and this amount is expected to drop to two workers per retiree by 2030.[10]

The program was stable when there were more than three workers per beneficiary. However, future projections indicate that the ratio will continue to fall from two workers to one, at which point the program in its current structure becomes financially unsustainable.[11] Of course, abortion would be morally wrong even if it were financially profitable for the country. The point is, abortion is not only morally wrong, but ultimately, also financially *un*profitable. By eliminating a large percentage of entire generations through legalized abortion, we've only compounded our society's problems.

The Wrong "Solution"

Among pro-life advocates there is honest debate about contraceptive use[12] and the degree to which people should strive to control the size of their families. But on the matter of controlling family size, we should all agree: *solutions based on killing a family member are not acceptable.*

Having endorsed abortion as a means of decreasing the number of the young, will society be compelled to use euthanasia as a means of reducing the old? Back in the 1980s, the governor of Colorado, Dick Lamm, told old people that rather than try to prolong their lives by expensive medical means, they had a duty to "step aside" (die). Given the pushback, public figures learned not to verbalize this outright, but the sentiment is still with us. If the elderly don't step aside, will society begin setting them aside? (That's an honest concern about today's "death with dignity" laws, which have legalized physician-assisted suicide in a number of U.S. states.)

After an Indiana infant called "Baby Doe" was legally allowed to die by decision of his parents, former Surgeon General C. Everett Koop publicly stated his fear that mandatory euthanasia would eventually result from the unwillingness of the younger generation to support the elderly. He said, "My fear is that one day for every Baby Doe in America, there will be ten thousand Grandma Does."

We should recognize that human beings are responsible for stewarding the earth and the natural resources we have available to us. So by all means, let's pursue smarter, better ways for people to care for the environment, wisely manage resources, produce food, and reduce poverty. But let's not buy into the lie that killing unborn children or the disabled or the elderly will improve our world's future.

"If abortion were made illegal, women would again die from unsafe abortions."

Because abortion has been legal in the U.S. for nearly fifty years, many wonder what would happen if it were outlawed nationwide. Would there continue to be many abortions, and would large numbers of women die in "back-alley" abortions performed with barbaric tools like clothes hangers, as pro-choice advocates claim?

First, that harmful acts against the innocent will take place regardless of the law *is a poor argument for having no law*. There are laws against burglary, rape, and armed robbery, yet every one of these crimes continues to happen in our society. Laws should discourage bad things from happening, not conform to them simply because they *do* happen.

So if, as we've seen in previous chapters in this book, the unborn child is in fact a person in an early stage of development, then he or she is a human being fully deserving of the protection of the law.

It's true that hearts and minds—not just laws—need to change in relation to abortion. Yet we often underestimate the power of law to mold thought as well as action. When slavery was abolished, people gradually began to think differently. The civil rights movement brought about further changes in law, and eventually in people's thinking. The law is a moral guide, a tutor that helps shape the conscience of society. As Martin Luther King, Jr. wrote, "Morality cannot be legislated, but behavior can be regulated. Judicial decrees may not change the heart, but they can restrain the heartless."[1]

The Law Led the Way

There were abortions in this country before abortion was legal, but the number skyrocketed once it was legalized. The Centers for Disease Control (CDC) reports that "from 1970 through 1982, the reported number of legal abortions in the United States increased every year."[2] Though the number of abortions in the United States peaked in 1990 at 1.6 million,[3] there were still approximately 862,320 abortions in the United States in 2017 (the most recent statistics available in 2020).[4] The laws that once restrained abortion now encourage it.

Former abortion-rights activist Bernard Nathanson admitted that he and his cofounders of NARAL (National Abortion Rights Action League) fabricated the figure that a million women were getting illegal abortions in America each year before *Roe v. Wade*. The average, he said, was actually one-tenth that number, about ninety-eight thousand per year. Nonetheless, the media eagerly disseminated the false information fed them by abortion activists.

The Truth about Maternal Deaths from Illegal Abortion

Nathanson also said that he and his associates invented the "nice, round shocking figure" of five to ten thousand women's deaths a year from illegal abortions.[5]

Research shows that in 1966, before the first state legalized abortion, a total of 120 mothers died from abortion.[6] The actual number of abortion deaths of women in the twenty-five years prior to 1973 averaged 250 a year, with a high of 388 in 1948.[7]

In 1972, abortion was still illegal in 80 percent of the country, but 63 reported deaths were attributed to complications of induced abortion. Of these deaths, 24 (38%) were associated with legal induced abortion and 39 (62%) with illegal induced abortion."

Suppose that only one out of five deaths from illegal abortion was properly identified. This would still mean that the number of women dying the year before abortion was legalized would be fewer than two hundred, only 2-4 percent of the five thousand to ten thousand per year claimed by pro-choice advocates.

This was not mere exaggeration. It was a complete fabrication, one still perpetuated today.

Maternal Deaths from Legal Abortion

Today, abortion is normally not life threatening to the mother. However, despite abortion's legality, the fatality rate is much higher than many pro-choice advocates admit. A widely disseminated pro-choice video produced in the late 1980s states, "By 1979 the Federal government could not identify a single woman anywhere in this country who died of abortion."[8]

This is an amazing statement, since many sources document a number of deaths from legal abortion. According to the *American Journal of Obstetrics and Gynecology,* "The New York City Department of Health reported seven legal abortion-related deaths that occurred between 1980 and 1985. The cause of death in all cases was attributed directly to general anesthesia."[9] In 1986, four doctors and researchers presented a study of no less than 193 deaths by legal abortion between 1972 and 1985.[10] According to the Centers for Disease Control and Prevention, 411 women have died from legal abortions from 1973 to 2009.[11] The fact that, despite a diligent search, we can't find any more current statistics on abortion deaths may reflect an unwillingness to divulge this information.

Since public health officials stopped looking for abortion-caused deaths after abortion became legal, the opportunity to overlook or cover up abortion-caused deaths is now much greater. What makes abortion-related deaths hard to trace is that the majority of the deaths do not occur during the surgery but afterward. Hence, any number of secondary reasons are routinely identified as the cause of death. I personally attended the memorial service of a woman who died from a legal abortion at an abortion clinic in Portland, Oregon. But this fact was not recognized in the newspaper coverage of her death.

A woman died in 2017 at a New Mexico abortion clinic while having a late-term abortion. Her official cause of death was listed as "pulmonary thromboembolism due to pregnancy."[12] In 2019, a woman died of a hemorrhage after having a first-term abortion at an Ohio abortion clinic. Another woman died at the same clinic in 2014, also of hemorrhaging, after a second-term abortion.[13]

In 2013, the nation was shocked by the horrific findings brought to light in the trial of Dr. Kermit Gosnell. The Philadelphia abortionist was ultimately charged with eight counts of murder for the deaths of several babies and one patient. The 2009 death of Karnamaya Mongar, who died after having an abortion at his clinic, did not trigger an investigation at the time.[14] (Another woman died in his care in 2002.)

Sarah Ruiz writes, "To say that abortion is a 'safe' procedure because it is legal is not only incorrect but dangerous. The mainstream media makes women think that abortion is no more serious than going in to get their teeth cleaned at the dentist. Women have died. Some have had irreparable damage to their bodies. Lives have been changed forever."[15]

Medical Equipment, Not Clothes Hangers

Since 90 percent of pre-1973 illegal abortions were done by physicians, it's safe to assume that even if abortion were outlawed, some physicians would continue to perform abortions (using modern medical equipment, not clothes hangers). Sadly, women would continue to have abortions. But many other women and children would be saved from the tragedy of abortion.

Clothes hangers make effective propaganda pieces at pro-choice rallies, but they do not accurately reflect what would happen if abortion were made illegal again. Clothes hangers would be used not for abortions, but for baby clothes.

The Central Horror of Illegal and Legal Abortion

We do not try to make kidnapping or child abuse or wife beating safe and legal. If abortion kills children, our goal should not be to make it as safe and legal as possible, but to provide compassionate alternatives and legal restrictions that help avoid it in the first place.

Unfortunately, every horror that was true of illegal abortion is also true of legal abortion. Abortion is horrible primarily because it's a process in which instruments of death invade a woman's body and kill her innocent child.

Neither laws nor slogans nor attractive waiting rooms nor advanced medical equipment can change the nature of abortion—the killing of children and the harming of their mothers.

"I'm personally pro-life, but a woman has a right to choose."

People commonly say, "I would never choose to have an abortion myself. But everyone's free to believe what they want, and I think women have the right to make their own choices. I won't impose my views on others."

Such statements reflect the illusion that being personally opposed to abortion while believing others should be free to choose is some kind of equitable compromise between the pro-abortion and pro-life positions. It isn't.

The biggest reason why this compromise doesn't work is spelled out in the phrase itself: "*personally opposed.*" Is an innocent *person* being killed by a woman's choice to have an abortion? If not, no problem. But if so, society—that means all of us—cannot afford to ignore or try to be neutral concerning this serious issue. Shouldn't we favor unborn persons having the right to live long enough to grow up and express their own personal opinions?

To the baby who dies, it makes no difference whether those who refused to protect her were *pro-abortion* or "merely" *pro-choice* about others having abortions. It's exactly the same outcome.

An Honest Confession

A radio talk show host once told me she was offended that some people called her "pro-abortion" instead of "pro-choice." I asked her, on the air, *Why don't you want to be called pro-abortion? Is there something wrong with abortion?"*

She responded, "Abortion is tough. It's not like anybody really wants one."

I said, "I don't get it. What makes it tough? Why wouldn't someone want an abortion?"

Frustrated, she said in an impassioned voice, "Well, you know, *it's a tough thing to kill your baby!"*

The second she said it, she caught herself, but it was too late. In an unguarded moment she'd revealed what she knew to be true. It's the same thing everyone knows if they'll only admit it: abortion is difficult for exactly the same reason it's wrong—*because it's killing a child.*

And when we're thinking clearly, we all know there is simply no justification for child-killing.

The only good reason to oppose abortion is a reason that compels us to say it should not be legal for others: because it takes away a child's most basic right—*his or her right to live.*

"Don't Like Slavery? Don't Own a Slave."

Francis Beckwith writes:

> If *you* believed that a class of persons were being murdered by methods that included dismemberment, suffocation, and burning, resulting in excruciating pain in many cases,

wouldn't you be perplexed if someone tried to ease your outrage by telling you that you didn't have to participate in the murders if you didn't want to? That's exactly what pro-lifers hear when abortion-rights supporters tell them, "Don't like abortion? Don't have one," or "I'm prochoice, but personally opposed to abortion." In the mind of the prolifer, this is like telling an abolitionist, "Don't like slavery, don't own a slave," or telling Dietrich Bonhoeffer, "Don't like the Holocaust, don't kill a Jew."[1]

Suppose Class A drug-dealing were legalized, as some have advocated. Then suppose you heard someone argue this way for selling cocaine:

I'm personally not in favor of drug deal-ing, but this is a matter for a drug dealer to decide between himself and his attorney. Lots of religious people are against drug dealing, but they have no right to force the anti-cocaine morality on others. We don't want to go back to the days when drug deal-ing was done in back alleys and people died from poorly mixed cocaine, and when only rich people could get drugs and poor people couldn't. It's better now that qualified drug dealers can safely give cocaine to our chil-dren. I personally wouldn't buy drugs, so I'm not pro-drugs, you understand, I'm just pro-choice about drug dealing.

In terms of moral impact, there is no significant difference between people who are in favor of drug dealing and people who don't like it personally but believe it should be legal. Someone who is pro-choice about rape might argue that this is not the same as being pro-rape. But what is the real difference? Wouldn't being pro-choice about rape allow and effectively promote the legitimacy of rape?

Being personally against abortion but favoring another's right to abortion is self-contradictory. It's exactly like saying, "I'm personally against child abuse, but I defend my neighbor's right to abuse his child if that is his choice."

Have you seen the bumper sticker with the slogan "Against Abortion? Don't Have One"? At first glance, it makes sense. The logic applies perfectly to piloting planes, playing football, or eating pizza . . . but *not* to rape, torture, kidnapping, or murder.

No Middle Ground

Many public figures are unapologetic in their support of abortion. Still, the "I personally oppose abortion, but... " position has historically been popular among politicians who want pro-life support because they don't feel good about abortion, and pro-choice support because they won't do anything to restrict abortion. My point is not simply that this position is irresponsible and cowardly, though I think it is. My point is that it is utterly illogical. Yet it isn't just politicians who say this. It's one of the most common abortion-related statements made. I know because I've often heard it.

It seems to me that the only good reason for personally opposing abortion is that it kills an innocent child. If it doesn't, there's no need to be against it. But if it does, then you should not just refrain from it yourself—you should oppose *others* doing it also. You should favor laws to restrict it, for exactly the same reason you favor laws to restrict rape, child molestation, and murder.

Abort73.com puts it this way:

> *I'm personally opposed to abortion, but people should be free to make their own choices.* If this is your attitude about abortion, if you think you've carved out some morally-neutral middle ground, ask yourself that same question in regard to slavery or lynching. Would you ever dare make the statement that, while you're personally opposed to lynching, you still support the rights of other men to lynch? If there was no middle ground in regard to slavery, there is no middle ground in regard to abortion. The reasons that the Supreme Court reversed itself about Dred Scott are the same reasons it should reverse itself about *Roe v. Wade*. Until they do, we continue to live in a society in which certain living persons are considered property.[2]

"Pro-life proponents are pro-birth, not pro-life. They only care about fetuses and do nothing to help children who are already born, as evidenced by how they vote."

Countless myths have been attached to the pro-life movement. One example is the oft-repeated statement, "Pro-lifers don't really care about pregnant women, or about children once they're born."

A television reporter, with cameras rolling, once approached me at a pro-life event and asked for my response to that accusation. I said, "Well, my wife and I opened our home to a pregnant girl and paid her expenses while she lived with us. We supported her when she decided to give up the child for adoption. And, since you asked, we give a substantial amount of our income to help poor women and children."

Then I introduced her to a pastor friend standing next to me who, with his wife, had adopted nineteen children, a number of them with Down syndrome and other special needs. The reporter signaled the cameraman to stop filming. I asked if she wanted to interview my friend. She shook her head and moved on, looking for someone who matched her stereotype.

A Word about the Word "Pro-Life"

First, let me say emphatically: pro-life people should be concerned not only for the unborn, but for the weak and needy, for the orphans and widows, for the hungry, for the abandoned and abused of all ages. We should fight against sex trafficking and racial injustice and the mistreatment of the elderly. We should obey God when he says, "Speak up for those who cannot speak for themselves, for the rights of all who are destitute. Speak up and judge fairly; defend the rights of the poor and needy" (Proverbs 31:8-9).

Being pro-life does not *end* with advocating for the protection of unborn children. However, because they are the smallest and weakest and most vulnerable human beings, and because they are killed at the highest rates and in the greatest numbers, and because countless people and even the law of the land argue for the right to destroy them, being pro-life certainly *begins* with defending the unborn.

Ironically, there are those who now use the term pro-life when it comes to the already born, but do little or nothing on behalf of the unborn. They have co-opted the term while abandoning its historic meaning. It would be like people in the mid-nineteenth century adopting the term "emancipation" to advocate for children working long hours in mines, while turning around and defending people's right to buy and sell slaves.

To be pro-life should certainly mean *more* than being concerned for unborn babies, but it should never mean *less* than that.

A Gigantic Grassroots Volunteer Movement

I do agree that people who point out injustice should seek to be part of the solution. Truthfully, that's already been happening for years in the pro-life cause. Thousands of pro-life organizations around the country and throughout the world provide free pregnancy tests, ultrasounds, counseling, support groups, childcare classes, financial management education, babysitting, diapers, children's clothes, and housing. To these, add tens of thousands of churches donating time, money, food, house repairs, and every other kind of help to needy pregnant women, single mothers, and low-income families. Countless pro-life families adopt children, open their homes, and volunteer to help children after they're born. Together, I am convinced these efforts actually comprise the single largest grassroots volunteer movement in history.

While those who offer abortions charge women for them, those who offer abortion alternatives give their assistance freely, lovingly, and almost entirely behind the scenes. Contrary to some caricatures, these people are not just pro-birth—they are truly pro-life. They care about a child and her mother, and help them both before birth and after.

Government Programs and Pro-Life Convictions

Pro-choice advocates sometimes say the proof that pro-life activists don't actually care about already-born children is found in how they vote and what government programs they do or don't support.

But a child's right to life is the foundational right from which all other rights flow, and that's why we have to start there. Nathan Apodaca writes, "The pro-life argument is that it's wrong to intentionally kill innocent human beings. Abortion does that. Therefore, abortion is wrong. How does my alleged rejection of big government programs and progressive political ideas refute that essential pro-life argument? It doesn't."[1]

Many pro-life advocates help women and children through charitable non-government means. Just because this help isn't directly connected to the government doesn't meant it isn't real and effective. (And in many cases, because non-government organizations are able to work more personally with individuals, they can be far *more* effective.)

Kyle Blanchette writes:

> …yes, there is something objectionable and inconsistent about someone whose pro-life activism amounts to nothing more than casting a vote for the candidate who opposes abortion, all the while refusing to lift a finger to help mothers and babies in difficult circumstances.
>
> But we must take care not to conflate help with government programs. Those opposed to abortion can both agree that mothers and babies deserve our help, and disagree that whatever government program

is under discussion is the best way to provide that help. Pro-lifers who care about mothers and babies, but who are also are skeptical of the efficiency and efficacy of some or all government programs, can be found giving to charities designed to help mothers and babies.[2]

Furthermore, regardless of who anyone votes for, all U.S. citizens pay taxes that support current government programs. "Since we are all subject to the same tax laws regardless of our stance on abortion or our faith in the efficacy of the programs that our taxes fund, all people (pro-life and pro-choice) support those programs to the same degree."[3] The vast amount given to pro-life causes is over and above, not in place of, the support to government programs inherent in paying taxes.

Some people believe we should make abortion "safe and rare" by supporting big-government programs that seek to address poverty and help women and families. They see this as a comprehensive pro-life solution, believing that if we can address the root of what causes women to choose abortion, we'll reduce its frequency. While it's certainly important for society to identify and work to address those root issues, and to help people in poverty, it's also fair to ask, "What kind of policy or program can address the plight of women facing unsupported pregnancy *without* supporting abortion?" Unfortunately, *any* support of the abortion industry, which has no financial interest in keeping abortion rare—in fact, quite the opposite—only bolsters it. (And if, as we've seen in previous chapters, abortion is the killing of an innocent child, then we wouldn't say, for example, "Let's work to make murder or child abuse safe and rare.")

There is room for legitimate debate and disagreement about various government programs, and how we can best help women and children in need. By all means, let's seek just and wise ways to do so. But the idea that the pro-life cause is hypocritical for not aligning with a specific list of political ideas and government programs is flawed. It can be either an *ad hominem* argument that unfairly attacks their character, or a straw man argument that falsely claims their lack of confidence in certain government programs proves they don't care about people.

The truth is, many pro-life people I know give generously not only to provide abortion alternatives but also to support organizations which effectively and efficiently feed the hungry and help the poor and needy in their communities and beyond.

"The Bible doesn't say anything against abortion, and many Christians believe it's acceptable."

In recent decades it has become popular for certain theologians and ministers to claim that conscientious Christians can be, or even should be, pro-choice. The Religious Coalition for Reproductive Choice, for instance, has adopted the motto, "Pro Faith. Pro Family. Pro Choice." It was formerly called the Religious Coalition for Abortion Rights, and their previous motto was, "Prayerfully Pro-Choice."

The arguments offered by these advocates are shallow, inconsistent, and violate the most basic principles of biblical interpretation.[1] The "Christian" pro-choice position is nothing more than an accommodation to modern secular beliefs, and it flies in the face of the Bible and the historical position of the church.

Some maintain that "nowhere does the Bible prohibit abortion."[2] Yet the Bible clearly prohibits the killing of innocent people (Exodus 20:13). All that is necessary to prove a biblical prohibition of abortion is to demonstrate that the Bible considers the unborn to be human beings.

Personhood in the Bible

A number of ancient societies opposed abortion,[3] but ancient Hebrew society had the clearest reasons for doing so because of its scriptural foundation. The Bible gives theological certainty to the biological evidence. It teaches that men and women are made in God's image (Genesis 1:27). Throughout Scripture, personhood is never measured by age, stage of development, or mental, physical, or social skills. Personhood is endowed by God at the moment of creation. That moment of creation can be nothing other than the moment of conception.

The Hebrew word used in the Old Testament to refer to the unborn (Exodus 21:22–25) is *yeled*, a word that "generally indicates young children, but may refer to teens or even young adults."[4] The Hebrews did not have or need a separate word for unborn children. They were just like any other children, only younger. In the Bible there are references to born children and unborn children, but there is no such thing as "potential," "incipient," or "almost" children.

Job graphically described the way God created him before he was born (Job 10:8–12). The person in the womb *was not something that might become Job, but someone who was* Job, just younger and smaller. God identifies Himself to Isaiah as, "he who made you, who formed you in the womb" (Isaiah 44:2). What each person is, not merely what he might become, was present in his mother's womb.

Psalm 139:13–16 paints a graphic picture of the intimate involvement of God with a preborn person. David says to his Creator, "You knit me together in my mother's womb." Each person has been personally knitted together by God. "All the days of his life have been planned out by God before any have come to be" (v. 16).

As a member of the human race that has rejected God, each person sinned "in Adam," and is therefore a sinner from his very beginning (Romans 5:12–19). David says, "Surely I was sinful at birth." Then he goes back even before birth to the actual beginning of his life, saying he was "sinful from the time my mother conceived me" (Psalm 51:5). Each person has a sin nature from the point of conception. Who but an actual person can have a moral nature? Rocks and trees and animals and human organs do not have moral natures, good or bad.

When Rebekah was pregnant with Jacob and Esau, Scripture says, "The babies jostled each other within her" (Genesis 25:22). The unborn are regarded as "babies" in the full sense of the term. God tells Jeremiah, "Before I formed you in the womb I knew you" (Jeremiah 1:5). He could not know Jeremiah in his mother's womb unless Jeremiah, the person, was present there.

In Luke 1:41 and 44 there are references to the unborn John the Baptist. The Greek word translated as "baby" in these verses is the word *brephos*. It is the same word used for the already born baby Jesus (Luke 2:12, 16) and for the babies brought to Jesus to receive His blessing (Luke 18:15–17). It is also the same word used in Acts 7:19 for the newborn babies killed by Pharaoh. To the writers of the New Testament, like the Old, a baby is simply a baby, whether born or unborn.

The angel Gabriel told Mary that she would be "with child and give birth to a son" (Luke 1:31). In the first century, and in every century, to be pregnant is to be with child, not with that which might become a child.

The Status of the Unborn

One scholar states: "Looking at Old Testament law from a proper cultural and historical context, it is evident that the life of the unborn is put on the same par as a person outside the womb."[5] Exodus 21:22–25 says, "If men struggle with each other and strike a woman with child so that she gives birth prematurely, yet there is no injury, he shall surely be fined as the woman's husband may demand of him, and he shall pay as the judges *decide*. But if there is *any further* injury, then you shall appoint *as a penalty* life for life, eye for eye, tooth for tooth, hand for hand, foot for foot, burn for burn, wound for wound, bruise for bruise" (NASB, emphasis added).

This passage is sometimes used as evidence that the unborn is subhuman. But a proper understanding of the passage shows the reference is not to a miscarriage, but to a premature birth, and that the "injury" referred to, which is to be compensated for, applies to the child as well as to his mother. This means that, "far from justifying permissive abortion, it in fact grants the unborn child a status in the eyes of the law equal to the mother's."[6]

Meredith Kline observes, "The most significant

thing about abortion legislation in Biblical law is that there is none. It was so unthinkable that an Israelite woman should desire an abortion that there was no need to mention this offense in the criminal code."[7] All that was necessary to prohibit an abortion was the command, "You shall not murder" (Exodus 20:13). Every Israelite knew that the pre-born child was indeed a child. Hence, miscarriage was viewed as the loss of a child, and abortion as the killing of a child.

Numbers 5:11–31 is an unusual passage used to make a central argument in a pro-choice Bible study book.[8] The authors cite the New English Bible's translation which makes it sound as if God brings a miscarriage on a woman if she is unfaithful to her husband. Other translations refer to a wasting of the thigh and a swelling of her abdomen. The CSB translates it "when he makes your womb shrivel and your belly swell" (Numbers 5:21). The ESV renders it "thigh fall away and your body swell." It's not at all certain a pregnancy is in mind.

It appears that God was expected to do some kind of miracle related to the bitter water, creating a dramatic physical reaction if adultery had been committed. The ESV Study Bible says, "…the guilty wife is threatened with childlessness, a catastrophe in Bible times, whereas the innocent is assured she shall be free and shall conceive children."[9]

The pro-choice Bible study suggests that if God indeed causes a miscarriage, it would be an endorsement of people causing abortions. This is a huge stretch, since neither the wife, the husband, nor the priest made the decision to induce an abortion. God is the creator of life and exercises rights over human life and death that He emphatically says we creatures do *not* (Exodus 20:13).

God and Miscarriages

Pro-choice advocates also use Hosea 9—which describes God's punishment against Israel for their idolatry and rejection of Him and talks about miscarriages—to make the claim that God is pro-abortion since he caused miscarriages. Verse 11 says, "Ephraim's glory shall fly away like a bird—no birth, no pregnancy, no conception!" and verse 14 says, "Give them, O Lord—what will you give? Give them a miscarrying womb and dry breasts."

The ESV Study Bible says this of Hosea 9:10-14:

> When Israel spurns God's grace, they are left to their own devices. Judgment is dramatic, for there will be no birth, no pregnancy, not even conception. If the nation does not change, it will soon head toward extinction. …A miscarrying womb would be the opposite of the fruitfulness the people sought in Baal worship.

Though God allowed these miscarriages as part of His judgment on Israel (and judgment is the key theme in this passage), these verses in Hosea do not endorse abortion. We will fail to understand this passage (and miscarriages in general) if we forget what bears repeating, that God has exclusive prerogatives over life and death that no human has:

"See now that I myself am He! There is no god besides me. I put to death and I bring to life, I have wounded and I will heal, and no one can deliver out of my hand." (Deuteronomy 32:39)

"The LORD brings death and makes alive; he brings down to the grave and raises up." (1 Samuel 2:6)

Still, some people make the argument that since there is a high rate of miscarriage in the natural reproductive process, God in essence "performs abortions." But the difference between spontaneous miscarriage and human-induced abortion is profound:

We did not start that tiny heart beating, create the blood that is flowing through the fetus's veins, or preordain the days of a child's life as God has done. Therefore, when human beings induce an abortion, we are destroying God's creative work without His permission. However, when God chooses, through miscarriage, to take a child's life early, He has the right to do so. It is His child, His work, His masterpiece (Ephesians 2:10; Mark 10:14).[10]

What God does is up to Him—and we are not God. Spontaneous miscarriages are not our responsibility. What *is* our responsibility is death caused by abortion.

God's love for children, and His oversight of each child's conception and birth, are clear truths from Scripture. Those truths are not antithetical to God's prerogatives over life and death.

Child Sacrifice

Child sacrifice is condemned throughout Scripture. Only the most degraded societies tolerated such evil. Ancient dumping grounds have been found filled with the bones of hundreds of dismembered infants. This is strikingly similar to discoveries of thousands of dead babies discarded by modern abortion clinics. One scholar of the ancient Near East refers to infant sacrifice as "the Canaanite counterpart to abortion."[11]

Scripture condemns the shedding of innocent blood (Deuteronomy 19:10; Proverbs 6:17; Isaiah 1:15; Jeremiah 22:17). While the killing of all innocent human beings is detestable, the Bible regards the killing of children as particularly heinous (Leviticus 18:21; 20:1–5; Deuteronomy 12:31).

Abortion and Church History

Christians throughout church history have affirmed with a united voice the humanity of the preborn child.[12] The second-century *Epistle of Barnabas* speaks of "killers of the child, who abort the mold of God." It treats the unborn child as any other human "neighbor" by saying, "You shall love your neighbor more than your own life. You shall not slay a child by abortion. You shall not kill that which has already been generated" (19.5).

The *Didache*, a second-century catechism for young converts, states, "Do not murder a child by abortion or kill a newborn infant" (2.2). Clement of Alexandria maintained that "those who use abortifacient medicines to hide their fornication cause not only the outright murder of the fetus, but of the whole human race as well" (*Paedagogus* 2.10.96.1).

Defending Christians before Marcus Aurelius in A.D. 177, Athenagoras argued, "What reason would we have to commit murder when we say that women who induce abortions are murderers, and will have to give account of it to God? . . . The fetus in the womb is a living being and therefore the object of God's care" (*A Plea for the Christians* 35.137–138).

Tertullian said, "It does not matter whether you take away a life that is born, or destroy one that is coming to the birth. In both instances, destruction is murder" (*Apology* 9.4). Basil the Great affirmed, "Those who give abortifacients for the destruction of a child conceived in the womb are murderers themselves, along with those receiving the poisons" (*Canons* 188.2). Jerome called abortion "the murder of an unborn child" (*Letter to Eustochium* 22.13).

Augustine warned against the terrible crime of "the murder of an unborn child" (*On Marriage* 1.17.15). Origen, Cyprian, and Chrysostom were among the many other prominent theologians and church leaders who condemned abortion as the killing of children. New Testament scholar Bruce Metzger comments, "It is really remarkable how uniform and how pronounced was the early Christian opposition to abortion."[13]

Throughout the centuries, Roman Catholic leaders have consistently upheld the sanctity of human life. Likewise, Protestant reformer John Calvin followed both the Scriptures and the historical position of the church when he affirmed:

> The fetus, though enclosed in the womb of its mother, is already a human being and it is a most monstrous crime to rob it of the life which it has not yet begun to enjoy. If it seems more horrible to kill a man in his own house than in a field, because a man's house is his place of most secure refuge, it ought surely to be deemed more atrocious to destroy a fetus in the womb before it has come to light.[14]

Modern theologians with a strong biblical orientation have normally agreed that abortion causes the death of a child. Dietrich Bonhoeffer, who lost his life standing against Hitler's murder of the innocent in Germany, argued that abortion is "nothing but murder."[15]

Theologian Karl Barth stated, "The unborn child is from the very first a child . . . it is a man and not a thing, not a mere part of the mother's body. . . . Those who live by mercy will always be disposed to practice mercy, especially to a human being which is so dependent on the mercy of others as the unborn child."[16]

The Bible and Children

The Bible is clear that every child in the womb is created by God. Furthermore, Christ loves that child and proved it by becoming like him—He spent nine months in His mother's womb. Finally, Christ died for that child, showing how precious He considers him to be.

The biblical view of children is that they are a gift from the Lord (Psalm 127:3–5). Yet society treats children more and more as liabilities. We must learn to see them as God does, and to act toward them as God commands us to act: "Defend the cause of the weak and fatherless; maintain the rights of the poor and oppressed. Rescue the weak and needy; deliver them from the hand of the wicked" (Psalm 82:3–4).

"How can I help save women and children from abortion?"

I f you consider yourself pro-choice, I commend you for reading all the way through this small book and actually hearing the pro-life position. I hope you grasp the significance of the evidence for the unborn child's humanity and therefore find conclusive reasons to oppose abortion.

In a science fiction story a spaceship crew member picks up a radio transmission of a little girl's voice. The girl is stranded on a dying planet. But the "Prime Directive," which binds the crew to a policy of noninterference, persuades them they cannot rescue the little girl. Only one crew member feels differently. That's the one who has actually heard her voice.

Just as they are about to leave her to die, the ship's officers receive another transmission. This time they *all* hear the girl's voice. Suddenly they change their minds. They realize that no matter what the cost, they *must* save this girl's life.

What has happened? The policy hasn't changed. The girl hasn't changed. Their knowledge of her dilemma hasn't changed. What has happened is that in their hearts they know what their heads had somehow failed to register—*this is indeed a little child who is about to die.* She is no longer a theory, but a fact.

Our willingness to come to grips with the fact that the unborn are real and precious little girls and boys—not just in theory, but in fact, not just in our heads but in our hearts—will largely determine what we will do for the children who are about to die.

However, what if you are still not convinced that every pregnancy involves a child? If you're driving through a neighborhood and see a cardboard box in the middle of the road that a child could fit into, wouldn't you avoid running over the box? Wouldn't you err on the side of life? If you have even the slightest doubt that someone could be harmed, surely the benefit of your doubt should go to human life, shouldn't it?

On the other hand, if you are now confident that abortion kills a living human being—a person worthy of protection—you might be wondering, "What am I supposed to do with this conviction? What difference can I possibly make?"

Years ago, a famine relief organization printed a poster with a photo of an emaciated woman and child that asked the question, "How do you feed a billion hungry people?" I stared at that poster, which stopped me in my tracks. The very thought of such immense needs is defeating, and could cause us to think, *It's impossible, so we shouldn't even try.* But then I saw at the bottom of the poster a powerful four-word answer: "One at a time."

That's how we can make a difference when it

comes to abortion—*one life at a time.* Here are five ways *you* can get involved.

Educate Yourself

Become thoroughly informed. Know the facts and the best responses to pro-choice arguments. Read and re-read all the chapters of this book. (Another great place to start is with the educational website Abort73,[1] which I've quoted.)Error! Hyperlink reference not valid.

Make yourself aware of the need that unplanned pregnancy and abortion creates. After taking time to learn about abortion, abstinence, adoption, and caring for needy women, pray for divine appointments where God can use you to make a difference in people's lives.

Perhaps you and your family have the means and opportunity to open your home to a pregnant woman who needs support and a place to live. Or perhaps you feel called to foster or adopt a child. Those are pro-life actions, and they *do* cumulatively make a difference, one person at a time.

Bring a Pro-Life Perspective

When appropriate, bring abortion issues into conversations and keep them visible in places such as blogs and social media. *Graciously* challenge others to rethink assumptions. Scripture says to speak up for those who cannot speak up for themselves (Proverbs 31:8–9). It helps when you have demonstrated your love for the people you are trying to convince.

Remember, vested interests, denial, and rationalization surround this topic. Someone may be pro-choice because they had abortions, recommended them, paid for them, or drove their girlfriend, wife, or daughter to get one and therefore may harbor personal reasons for not wanting to believe abortion kills children. We should approach this tender subject in a Christ-like manner, displaying both grace and truth (see John 1:14).

You can also talk to your children and grandchildren about the sanctity of life and the humanity of the unborn. By teaching and modeling love for people and children of all ages, we pass on a pro-life worldview to future generations.

Support Pro-Life Organizations

You might consider spearheading a pro-life ministry in your church, or finding one in your area.[2] Donate time, money, equipment, clothes, or professional skills to pregnancy centers, adoption ministries, women's homes, abstinence agencies, right-to-life educational and political organizations, and other pro-life groups. Perhaps you could mow their lawn, clean their office, or repair their driveway, copiers, or plumbing. Or perhaps design or maintain their website or fix their computers.

We can all offer our God-given resources to the Lord. Ask God to show you the unique ways He has for *you* to contribute to helping. He *will* use your skills and funds to make a difference. Ask yourself: "What has God given me? How can I use that to help touch lives?"

Years ago a friend of mine used his construction skills to remodel the house that became the pregnancy resource center in my hometown. This man, whose size rivals an NFL lineman's, might not be the first choice to counsel a pregnant woman, but the work of his hands has had eternal impact on literally thousands of women and children.

Intervene Outside an Abortion Clinic

Consider peacefully praying, holding signs, and sharing pro-life information, as well as the gospel, outside an abortion clinic.

A pastor once shared a heartbreaking story about a post-abortive woman he had counseled. As she was leaving his office, he asked her, "If there would have been anyone outside the clinic when you went to get your abortion, what would you have done?" She said that before she left her house she had decided that if there was anyone standing outside the clinic in opposition, she wouldn't go ahead with the abortion. Tragically, there was no one there. This woman's story—which likely isn't unique to her—vividly demonstrates our need to act.

Denny Hartford, director of Vital Signs Ministries, writes: "Does prayer at the abortion centers and sidewalk counseling matter? You better believe it! From testimonies received over the years (including from former abortionists), we are convinced that God is accomplishing great things by our peaceful, prayerful presence at the abortion clinics."

When people see you standing up for the rights of the unborn, those with hard hearts will resent you. But those whose hearts are being softened by God's Spirit are interested and may genuinely listen. They may be open not just when you talk about the unborn and the beauty of life, but also when you talk about Jesus. And if someone doesn't like you, so what? In the final day each of us will stand before the Audience of One. It won't matter what others thought and said about us.

There are ministries such as Sidewalk Advocates for Life that can testify to the effectiveness of what is called sidewalk advocacy:

> We have seen abundant miracles when people show up to pray and peacefully reach out to those going into the abortion center. Many of us have kept in touch with mothers we have served, and some of us have actually met the children who have been saved by God's grace!
>
> Quite often, the only thing a woman in an unplanned pregnancy needs to hear is, "We're here to help you." ...Are there people who refuse to take your offer of help? Absolutely. But we believe that it still makes a difference that we are there to pray for those families and stand for preborn children and our community.[3]

Life advocates don't just try to stop abortions. The law of love also motivates us to provide money, housing, baby clothes, adoption services, legal help, counseling, and a myriad of other forms of support to pregnant women.

Pray

Finally, pray regularly for pro-life ministries, churches, mothers, babies, and those who work in the abortion industry. Overcoming the darkness of child-killing requires spiritual warfare, fought with humble and persistent prayer (Ephesians 6:10–20). Perhaps you might organize a prayer group of likeminded people in your community or at your church.

Some encouraging advancements have surfaced on the pro-life front. The number of abortions in the United States has steadily declined since the 1990s.[4] I believe the pro-life movement, made up of individuals giving of their time, resources, money, and effort, can take a lot of credit for this decline. At the same time, we must realize there are more chemical abortions than ever, and we must do more to educate people about this sad reality.[5]

Still, every day, on average, there are over 2,000 abortions performed in the U.S. There's much work to be done—and the good news is that every one of us can do something. May we, in our hearts and actions, have mercy on the smallest and weakest of God's precious children, and reach out in love and compassion to their mothers.

The Historic Connection between Racism and Abortion

I am painfully aware that advocates and opponents of nearly every cause misquote or misrepresent the facts, or take them out of context. I have seen both the pro-life and pro-choice camps do this, and I have seen both quote unreliable sources.

I say this because I am including facts in this appendix that would have distracted from the main book, but which are nonetheless important for those who wish to understand the history of the abortion rights movement in its early years, and how its beliefs and values carried over to the founding of Planned Parenthood, the world's leading abortion provider and promoter.

To some this may appear like those slanderous internet hoaxes full of false claims. I understand that concern, because I too cringe at such things. When I first heard people talk, thirty years ago, about the roots of Planned Parenthood and the beliefs of Margaret Sanger, I didn't believe them. I saw quotations in books, but how could I know if they were accurate? So I went to the largest library in Oregon in hopes of finding the original sources. I did, and read through those original documents myself. Every quotation you will see below is word for word from the primary source, not from secondary ones.

Margaret Sanger was the direction-setter and first president of Planned Parenthood. Under her leadership, Planned Parenthood ended up viewing abortion as one more means of controlling the birthrate of those considered inferior. Thirty years ago, in that library, I wrote, "I have in front of me a stack of Sanger's original writings, as well as copies of her magazine, *Birth Control Review*. I encourage readers to review these writings and decide for themselves the beliefs and attitudes that gave birth to Planned Parenthood and the American abortion movement."

Margaret Sanger spoke of the poor and handicapped as the "sinister forces of the hordes of irresponsibility and imbecility," claiming their existence constituted an "attack upon the stocks of intelligence and racial health."[1] She warned of "indiscriminate breeding" among the less fit that would bring into the world future voters "who may destroy our liberties, and who may thus be the most far-reaching peril to the future of civilization."[2] She called the less privileged members of society "a dead weight of human waste."[3]

In a chapter called the "Cruelty of Charity," Sanger argued that groups dedicated to helping pregnant women decide to give birth to their children were "positively injurious to the community and the future of the race."[4] She claimed, "The effect of maternity endowments and maternity centers supported by private philanthropy would have, perhaps already have had, exactly the most dysgenic tendency."[5] Her use of the technical term *dysgenic* clearly indicates her belief that efforts to support these women violated Darwin's doctrine of the survival of the fittest, by which the weaker were naturally eliminated because of their inferiority.

This same spirit permeates Sanger's magazine, *Birth Control Review*. It is full of articles with titles such as "The World's Racial Problem," "Toward Race Betterment," and "Eugenic Sterilization: An Urgent Need."[6] The latter article was written in 1933 by Dr. Ernst Rudin, a leader in the German eugenics movement that was at the time busily laying the foundation for the Nazi's acts of "racial improvement" and "ethnic cleansing." (This isn't speculation or exaggeration; it's an historical fact.)

Elsewhere in that issue an article titled "Defective Families" calls the "American Gypsies" a "family of degenerates" started by a man and "a half-breed woman," and warns that "their germ plasm has been traced throughout seven middle-western states."[7] Also in the same issue, in his article "Birth Control and Sterilization," Sanger's associate and lover, Dr. Havelock Ellis, stated, "Sterilization would be... helpful, although it could not be possible in this way to eliminate the mentally unfit element in the population. It would only be a beginning."[8] Students of history know where that "beginning" ended only a decade later, under the leadership of a eugenic devotee name Adolf Hitler. (Though Sanger did not write these specific articles herself, as founder and director she was responsible for the magazine's content and the ideas it promoted.)

The international eugenics movement, of which Margaret Sanger was inarguably a part, openly praised Nazi racial policies at least as late as 1938. Sanger gave the welcoming address to a 1925 international eugenics conference.

According to Marvin Olasky, Margaret Sanger's "Negro Project" of the 1930s was "hailed for its work in spreading contraception among those whom eugenicists most deeply feared."[9] When it became evident that contraceptives were not sufficiently curtailing the black population and other target groups, the eugenicists turned to abortion as a solution to the spread of unwanted races and families.

In Margaret Sanger's own words, to help the weaker and less privileged survive and to allow them to reproduce was to take a step backward in human evolution: "Instead of decreasing and aiming to eliminate the stocks that are most detrimental to the future of the race and the world, it tends to render them to a menacing degree dominant."[10]

These "stocks" were the poor and uneducated, a large portion of whom were ethnic minorities. Sanger was more interested in "aiming to eliminate" these "stocks" (read *people*) than in helping them. (In keeping with what we saw in Claim #2 of this book, a key part of the dehumanizing of people was the semantic manipulation that used other terms such as "stocks," normally used of cattle and other animals. The same applies to use of words like *tissue*, *cluster of cells*, and even *fetus* as a way of avoiding the word *child*, which connotes personhood.)

This history helps to explain why to this day Planned Parenthood does virtually nothing to promote adoption or to help poor and minority women who choose to give their children life rather than abort them. In fact, the organization targets inner-city areas with predominant minorities to establish their clinics. It also partly explains why abortion rates among minorities are dramatically higher than among whites. The Guttmacher Institute says that the abortion rate per 1,000 women aged 15-44 in America is 10% among whites, 18.1% among Hispanics, and 27.1% among blacks.[11]

BlackGenocide.org shares these statistics about the effects of abortion on the Black community:

On average, 1,876 black babies are aborted every day in the United States.

This incidence of abortion has resulted in a tremendous loss of life. It has been estimated that since 1973 Black women have had about 16 million abortions. Michael Novak had calculated "Since the number of current living Blacks (in the U.S.) is 36 million, the missing 16 million represents an enormous loss, for without abortion, America's Black community would now number 52 million persons. It would be 36 percent larger than it is. Abortion has swept through the Black community like a scythe, cutting down every fourth member."[12]

The Guttmacher Institute website, at the time of this writing (2020) features the words "Abortion is essential health care. Always." They believe Planned Parenthood (who owns them) performs abortion as an empowering and liberating service. Hence, they appear quite proud of the fact that they kill nearly twice as many Hispanic children as white, and nearly three times as many black children. Of course, Planned Parenthood today would never use the ugly language of Margaret Sanger. But surely it's fair to say that if Sanger were alive today, given her racial and eugenic prejudices, she would surely applaud this dramatic racial disparity when it comes to abortion. The fact that there are some highly visible blacks and other minority leaders in Planned Parenthood does not change its heritage or philosophy. It simply makes it easier to carry out its policies among target groups.

How devoted is Planned Parenthood to eliminating their competitors? They frequently attack alternative pregnancy centers, which give women other choices besides abortion, through restrictive legislation and other means. Why do they see pregnancy centers that offer free ultrasounds as threatening them? Why are they so determined that women, including the many minority women who enter their clinics, not be allowed to see the ultrasound images of the children living inside of them? Why do they oppose women being able to see and hear the medical facts and make an informed choice about whether or not to take the lives of their children?

Though I have read many Planned Parenthood materials, I had never until July 2020 seen any that renounced or apologized for Sanger's blatant eugenicism, her bias against the poor and the mentally and physically handicapped, and her racism, all of which characterized Planned Parenthood's philosophy from its inception.[13] While it was good that Planned Parenthood, to some extent, finally admitted what had been true for nearly one hundred years and which some of us had documented thirty years ago, my question is what will Planned Parenthood do now? Will they stop targeting black neighborhoods with their clinics, or will they continue to do so in the name of "serving the African-American community"? In other words, will they keep fulfilling Margaret Sanger's eugenic racism of eliminating "undesirable" minority children while publicly distancing themselves from it?

I do not believe Margaret Sanger was insincere or incorrect in everything she said and did. Nor do I believe most people who support abortion rights are racists, any more than I believe there are no racists among pro-lifers. I *do* believe that regardless of motives, a closer look at both the history and present strategies of the pro-choice movement suggests that "abortion for the minorities" may not serve the cause of racial equality as much as the cause of white supremacy.

Facing an unplanned pregnancy?

You need to know you have real and life-giving options, and there is so much hope!

Find a pregnancy center near you at:
resources.care-net.org/find-a-pregnancy-center

Or contact OptionLine by calling 1-800-712-4357, texting "HELPLINE" to 313131, or starting a chat at optionline.org

Looking for hope and healing after an abortion?

Millions of women and men, both in society and in the church, are suffering under the guilt of abortion.

Learn more about the hope Christ offers you at epm.org/abortionforgiveness

Find more help and resources by
contacting Support After Abortion at
supportafterabortion.com

ABOUT THE AUTHOR

Randy Alcorn is an author and the founder and director of Eternal Perspective Ministries (EPM), a nonprofit ministry dedicated to teaching principles of God's Word and assisting the church in ministering to the unreached, unfed, unborn, uneducated, unreconciled, and unsupported people around the world. His ministry focus is communicating the strategic importance of using our earthly time, money, possessions and opportunities to invest in need-meeting ministries that count for eternity. He accomplishes this by analyzing, teaching, and applying biblical truth.

Before starting EPM in 1990, Randy served as a pastor for fourteen years. He has a Bachelor of Theology and Master of Arts in Biblical Studies from Multnomah University and an Honorary Doctorate from Western Seminary in Portland, Oregon and has taught on the adjunct faculties of both.

A *New York Times* bestselling author of over 50 books, including *Heaven* (over one million sold), *The Treasure Principle* (over two million sold), *If God Is Good, Happiness,* and the award-winning novel *Safely Home.* His books sold exceed eleven million copies and have been translated into over seventy languages.

Randy resides in Gresham, Oregon, with his wife, Nanci. They have two married daughters and five grandsons. Randy enjoys hanging out with his family, biking, underwater photography, research, listening to audiobooks, and reading.

Connect with Randy online:

Facebook: facebook.com/randyalcorn
Twitter: twitter.com/randyalcorn
Blog: epm.org/blog

See a full list of Randy's books at
epm.org/books

NOTES

Introduction

1 Guttmacher Institute, "Induced Abortion in the United States," September 2019, https://www.guttmacher.org/fact-sheet/induced-abortion-united-states.

2 Ibid.

3 Guttmacher Institute, "Induced Abortion Worldwide," May 2016, https://www.guttmacher.org/fact-sheet/facts-induced-abortion-worldwide.

4 Gallup, "Majority in U.S. Still Want Abortion Legal, With Limits," June 25, 2019, https://news.gallup.com/poll/259061/majority-abortion-legal-limits.aspx.

5 National Right to Life, "The State of Abortion in the United States, 2019," January 2019, https://www.nrlc.org/uploads/communications/stateofabortion2019.pdf.

Pro-Choice Claim #1

1 David Reardon, *Aborted Women: Silent No More* (Westchester, IL: Crossway Books, 1987), 250.

2 Ibid.

3 Maureen L. Condic, "Life: Defining the Beginning by the End," First Things, May 2003, http://www.firstthings.com/article/2003/05/life-defining-the-beginning-by-the-end.

4 Ibid.

5 Ibid.

6 R. Houwink, *Data: Mirrors of Science* (New York: American Elsevier, 1970), 104–90.

7 Chemicals designated A, C, T & G form the basis for all DNA with variations in the order of the chemicals resulting in cell specialization and tissue differentiation. http://

137

web.ornl.gov/sci/techresources/Human_Genome
/project/index.shtml.

8 "The Facts of Life" (Norcross, GA: Human Development
   Resource Council), 2.

9 Annie Murphy Paul, "The First Ache," *The New York Times
   Magazine*, February 10, 2008, http://nyti.ms/1T0rf7z.

10 See "The War over Fetal Rights," *Newsweek*, 9 June 2003,
   40–47.

11 These are well-established scientific facts. See, e.g.,
   Landrum Shettles and David Rorvik, *Rites of Life* (Grand
   Rapids, MI: Zondervan, 1983), 41–66.

Pro-Choice Claim #2

1 Cited in Liz Klimas, "Ethicists Argue in Favor of 'After-
   birth Abortions,' as Newborns Are 'Not Persons,'" The
   Blaze, February 27, 2012, http://www.theblaze.com
   /stories/ethicists-argue-in-favor-of-after-birth-abortions
   -as-newborns-are-not-persons/.

2 Roe v. Wade, 410 U.S. (1973).

3 Ibid.

4 Peter Singer, *Practical Ethics* (Cambridge, UK: Cambridge
   University Press, 1979).

5 Peter Singer, "Sanctity of Life or Quality of Life," *Pediat-
   rics*, July 1983, 129.

6 Singer, "Taking Life: Humans," http://www.petersinger-
   links.com/taking.htm; excerpted from Singer, *Practical
   Ethics* (New York: Cambridge University Press, 1993).

7 Charles Hartshorne, "Concerning Abortion: An Attempt
   at a Rational View," *The Christian Century*, 21 January
   1981, 42-45.

8 Doug Criss, "A parent killing a child happens more often
   than we think," CNN.com, July 7, 2017, https://www.
   cnn.com/2017/07/07/health/filicide-parents-killing-kids-
   stats-trnd/index.html.

9 Peter Singer, *Rethinking Life and Death* (New York: St.
   Martin's Griffin, 1996), 217.

10 Dr. Seuss, *Horton Hears a Who* (New York: Random House, 1954), multiple pages.

11 Joseph Fletcher, *Situation Ethics: The New Morality*, cited by Mark O'Keefe, "Personhood: When Does It Begin...or End?" *Oregonian*, 12 February 1995, B1.

12 Maureen L. Condic, "Life: Defining the Beginning by the End," First Things, May 2003, http://www.firstthings.com /article/2003/05/life-defining-the-beginning-by-the-end.

13 Jonathan Leeman and Matthew Arbo, "Why Abortion Makes Sense," The Gospel Coalition, June 1, 2016, https:// www.thegospelcoalition.org/article/why-abortion -makes-sense.

Pro-Choice Claim #3

1 Warren M. Hern, *Abortion Practice* (Philadelphia: J.B. Lippincott Company, 1990), 14.

2 Michael Spielman, "Publicly Aborting Twins on Instagram," Abort73, September 12, 2014, http://abort73.com /blog/publicly_aborting_twins_on_instagram/.

3 Jia Tolentino, "The Messiness of Reproduction and the Dishonesty of Anti-Abortion Propaganda," *The New Yorker*, May 17, 2019, https://www.newyorker.com /culture/cultural-comment/the-messiness-of-reproduction -and-the-dishonesty-of-anti-abortion-propaganda.

4 Judith Jarvis Thomson, "A Defense of Abortion," *Philosophy and Public Affairs*, Volume 1, No. 1, Autumn 1971, 47–66.

5 Greg Koukl, "Unstringing the Violinist," Stand to Reason, https://www.str.org/articles/unstringing-the-violinist#. Xi8k5TJKj-g.

6 Ibid.

7 Scott Klusendorf, *The Case for Life*, (Wheaton, IL: Crossway Books, 2009), 188.

8 John W. Kennedy, "The Hidden Holocaust," *Power for Living*, 8 January 2009, 7.

Pro-Choice Claim #4

1 Mary O'Brien Drum, "Meeting in the Radical Middle," *Sojourners*, November 1980, 23.

2   https://www.americanadoptions.com/pregnant/waiting
    _adoptive_families.

3   Mortimer J. Adler, *Haves Without Have-Nots: Essays for
    the 21st Century on Democracy and Socialism* (New York:
    Macmillan, 1991), 210.

4   Jim Newhall, cited in Maureen O'Hagan, "Cross Hairs to
    Bear," *Willamette Week*, 3 May 1995.

5   Cited by John Leo in "The Moral Complexity of Choice,"
    U.S. News & World Report, 11 December 1989, 64.

6   Ibid.

Pro-Choice Claim #5

1   NARAL Pro-Choice America, "Abortion Access," accessed
    December 24, 2019, https://www.prochoiceamerica.org
    /issue/abortion-access/.

2   R. C. Sproul, *Abortion: A Rational Look at an Emotional
    Issue,* (Colorado Springs, CO: NavPress, 1990), 117–8.

3   Mary E. John, Ravinder Kaur, Rajni Palriwala, Saras-
    wati Raju and Alpana Sagar, "Disappearing Daughters,"
    ActionAid UK, accessed December 24, 2019, http://www.
    actionaid.org.uk/sites/default/files/doc_lib/disappearing
    _daughters_0608.pdf.

4   UNFPA (United Nations Population Fund), "Gender-
    biased sex selection," accessed December 24, 2019,
    https://www.unfpa.org/gender-biased-sex-selection.

5   Anna Higgins, J.D., "Sex-Selection Abortion: The Real
    War on Women," The Charlotte Lozier Institute, April 13,
    2016, https://lozierinstitute.org/sex-selection-abortion
    -the-real-war-on-women/.

6   Frederica Mathewes-Green, *Real Choices* (Sisters, OR:
    Multnomah Publishers, 1995), 19.

7   Elizabeth Ring-Cassidy and Ian Gentles, *Women's Health
    after Abortion: The Medical and Psychological Evidence,* 2nd
    ed. (Toronto: deVeber Institute, 2003), www.deveber.org.

8   Priscilla Coleman, "Abortion and Mental Health: Quan-
    titative Synthesis and Analysis of Research Published

1995–2009," *British Journal of Psychiatry,* 199, September 2011, http://bjp.rcpsych.org/content/199/3/180.abstract.

9 Joseph A. D'Agostino, "Abortion Causes Massive Mental Health Problems for Women," *Human Events,* January 30, 2006, https://humanevents.com/2006/01/30/abortion-causes-massive-mental-health-problems-for-women/.

10 Angela Lanfranchi, MD, "The Science, Studies and Sociology of the Abortion Breast Cancer Link," *Association for Interdisciplinary Research in Values and Social Change Research Bulletin* 18, no. 2, Spring 2005, https://www.questia.com/library/journal/1P3-942266431/the-science-studies-and-sociology-of-the-abortion.

11 Elizabeth Shadigian, MD, testimony before the Senate subcommittee on science, technology, and space's hearing to investigate the physical and psychological effects of abortion on women; cited in "Witnesses Ask U.S. Senate for Research into Side Effects of Abortion on Women," *Culture & Cosmos* 1, Number 30, March 9, 2004.

12 Lars Heisterberg, MD, et al., "Sequelae of Induced First-Trimester Abortion," *American Journal of Obstetrics and Gynecology,* July 1986, 79.

13 F. Parazzini et al., "Reproductive Factors and the Risk of Invasive and Intraepithelial Cervical Neoplasia," *British Journal of Cancer* 59, 1989, 805–9; H. L. Stewart et al., "Epidemiology of Cancers of the Uterine Cervix and Corpus, Breast and Ovary in Israel and New York City," *Journal of the National Cancer Institute* 37, Number 1:1–96; I. Fujimoto et al., "Epidemiologic Study of Carcinoma in Situ of the Cervix," *Journal of Reproductive Medicine* 30, Number 7, July 1985, 535; C. LaVecchia et al., "Reproductive Factors and the Risk of Hepatocellular Carcinoma in Women," *International Journal of Cancer* 52, 1992, 351.

14 Joel Brind, "Comprehensive Review and Meta-Analysis of the Abortion/Breast Cancer Link," https://www.ncbi.nlm.nih.gov/pmc/articles/PMC1060338/pdf/jepicomh00185-0007.pdf.

15 L. A. Brinton et al., "Reproductive Factors in the Aetiology of Breast Cancer," *British Journal of Cancer* 47, 1983, 757–62. https://www.ncbi.nlm.nih.gov/pubmed/6860545.

16 "Summary of Women's Health After Abortion: Abortion and Breast Cancer," The deVeber Institute for Bioethics and Social Research, accessed December 26, 2019, https://www.deveber.org/womens-health-after-abortion/.

17 American Cancer Society, "Abortion and Cancer Risk," June 19, 2014, https://www.cancer.org/cancer/cancer-causes/medical-treatments/abortion-and-breast-cancer-risk.html.

18 "The Health Consequences of Sex Trafficking and Their Implications for Identifying Victims in Healthcare Facilities," Lederer, L., Wetzel, C. A. Annals of Health Law, Volume 23, Issue 1, 61-91, 2014.

19 Live Action, "Aiding Abusers: Planned Parenthood's cover-up of child sexual abuse," May 2018, https://www.liveaction.org/wp-content/uploads/2018/05/Planned%20Parenthood%20Sexual%20Abuse%20Report%202018.pdf.

20 Wagatwe Wanjuki, "The Pro-Life Movement Is Driven by Bigotry, Not Babies," *Dame Magazine*, May 29, 2019, https://www.damemagazine.com/2019/05/29/the-pro-life-movement-is-driven-by-bigotry-not-babies/.

Pro-Choice Claim #6

1 Marvin Olasky, "The Village's Prolife Voice," *Christianity Today*, 24 June 1991, 24.

2 Ibid, 24–6.

3 Nat Hentoff, "Pro-choice bigots: a view from the pro-life left," November 30, 1992, http://groups.csail.mit.edu/mac/users/rauch/nvp/consistent/hentoff_pro-life_left.html.

4 Pro-Life Humanists, "About Pro-Life Humanists," www.prolifehumanists.org.

5 Kristine Kruszelnicki, "Yes, There Are Pro-Life Atheists Out There. Here's Why I'm One of Them," Friendly

Atheist, March 11, 2014, www.patheos.com/blogs/friend-lyatheist/2014/03/11/yes-there-are-pro-life-atheists-out-there-heres-why-im-one-of-them.

6   Marist Poll, "Abortion in America," January 2015, www.kofc.org/un/en/resources/communications/Abortion_in_America_January2015_For_Release_150121.pdf.

7   Landrum Shettles and David Rorvik, Rites of Life (Grand Rapids, MI: Zondervan Publishing House, 1983), 103.

8   Bernard N. Nathanson, "Deeper into Abortion," *New England Journal of Medicine*, 291, 1974, 1189–90.

9   Bernard Nathanson, *Aborting America*, (New York: Doubleday, 1979), 227.

Pro-Choice Claim #7

1   Lawrence B. Finer, et al., Guttmacher Institute, "Reasons U.S. Women Have Abortions; Quantitative and Qualitative Perspectives," Vol. 37, No 3, Sept 2005, http://www.guttmacher.org/pubs/journals/3711005.pdf. (Guttmacher Institute, which is the research arm of Planned Parenthood, does not appear to offer up-to-date information on abortion statistics. The studies we cite are the most recent ones available as of December 2019.)

2   Sue Owen, "Surveys show wide disagreement on number of rape-related pregnancies per year," *Politifact Texas*, August 15, 2013, https://www.politifact.com/texas/statements/2013/aug/15/wendy-davis/surveys-show-wide-disagreement-number-rape-related/.

3   *Feminists for Life Debate Handbook* (Kansas City, MO: Feminists for Life of America, n.d.), 14.

4   Ryan Bomberger, "Conceived in rape, I am the 1 percent used to justify 100 percent of abortions," *Life Site News*, May 20, 2019, https://www.lifesitenews.com/opinion/conceived-in-rape-i-am-the-1-percent-used-to-justify-100-percent-of-abortions.

5   See "Finding Forgiveness After an Abortion," https://www.epm.org/resources/2010/Jan/21/finding-forgiveness-after-abortion/.

6   Hilary White, "No Case Where Abortion Was 'Necessary
     to Save Mom': Eminent Irish Oncologist," *Life Site News,*
     February 22, 2012, https://www.lifesitenews.com/news
     /no-case-where-abortion-was-necessary-to-save-mom
     -eminent-irish-oncologist.

7   "There Is a High Chance of Two Happy Outcomes," *Irish
     Independent,* December 16, 2011, https://www.independ-
     ent.ie/life/family/mothers-babies/there-is-a-high-chance-of
     -two-happy-outcomes-26803124.html.

8   Omar L. Hamada, MD, Twitter, January 23, 2019.

9   Elyce Cardonick, "Pregnancy-Associated Breast Cancer:
     Optimal Treatment Options." International Journal of
     Women's Health. Dove Medical Press, November 4, 2014.
     https://www.ncbi.nlm.nih.gov/pmc/articles/PMC4226455/.

Pro-Choice Claim #8

1   Planned Parenthood Federation of America, "Born
     Unwanted: Developmental Consequences for Children of
     Unwanted Pregnancies."

2   American Adoptions, "How Many Couples are Waiting
     to Adopt?," accessed December 19, 2019, https://www.
     american
     adoptions.com/pregnant/waiting_adoptive_families.

3   Abort73, "Common Abortion Fallacies," accessed Septem-
     ber 1, 2017, http://www.abort73.com/abortion/common
     _objections/.

4   US Department of Health and Human Services, "Report
     of the National Center of Child Abuse and Neglect,"
     1973–1982.

5   US Department of Health and Human Services, "Child
     Maltreatment 2017," accessed December 19, 2019,
     https://www.acf.hhs.gov/sites/default/files/cb/cm2017.pdf.

Pro-Choice Claim #9

1   Micaiah Bilger , "Planned Parenthood Annual Report
     Shows It Killed 332,757 Babies in Abortions, More Than
     Ever Before," LifeNews.com, January 21, 2019, https://

www.lifenews.com/2019/01/21/planned-parenthood
-annual-report-shows-it-killed-332757-babies-in-abortions
-more-than-ever-before/.

2   Maria Baer, "Most Abortion-Minded Women Aren't
    Calculating Killers. They're Afraid," The Gospel Coalition,
    May 16, 2019, https://www.thegospelcoalition.org/article
    /women-abortions-devious-murderers/.

3   Micaiah Bilger, "She Rejected Abortion After Getting Preg-
    nant in High School, Now She Helps Other Teens Choose
    Life," LifeNews.com, November 25, 2016, https://www.
    lifenews.com/2016/11/25/she-rejected-abortion
    -after-getting-pregnant-in-high-school-now-she-helps
    -other-teens-choose-life/.

4   "What if her partner, friends or family have abandoned
    her? Or what if she is poor?," Feminists for Life, accessed
    December 27, 2019, https://www.feministsforlife.org
    /what-if-her-partner-friends-or-family-have-abandoned
    -her-or-what-if-she-is-poor/.

5   Cited by Charmaine Yoest, "Why Is Adoption So Diffi-
    cult?" Focus on the Family Citizen, 17 December 1990, 10.

6   Maria Baer, "Most Abortion-Minded Women Aren't
    Calculating Killers. They're Afraid," The Gospel Coalition,
    May 16, 2019, https://www.thegospelcoalition.org/article
    /women-abortions-devious-murderers/.

Pro-Choice Claim #10

1   Lyndsay Werking-Yip, "I Had a Late-Term Abortion. I
    Am Not a Monster," The New York Times, October 19,
    2019, https://www.nytimes.com/2019/10/19/opinion
    /sunday/late-term-abortion.html.

2   Aimee Green, "Jury awards nearly $3 million to Portland-
    area couple in 'wrongful birth' lawsuit against Legacy
    Health," Oregon Live, March 9, 2012, https://www.oregon
    live.com/portland/2012/03/jury_rules_in_portland-area
    _co.html.

3   Laura Nicole, "Aborting babies with disabilities is a tragedy,
    not an act of compassion," Live Action, October 28, 2019,

https://www.liveaction.org/news/aborting-babies
-disabilities-tragedy-not-act-compassion/.

4   75 percent of babies with anencephaly are live births.
    See Monika Jaquier, "Report about the Birth and Life of
    Babies with Anencephaly," Anancephalie.info, March 7,
    2006, https://www.anencephaly.info/e/report.php.

5   Anencephaly.Info, "Jesse Alexander Brand,"October 10,
    2007, https://www.anencephaly.info/e/jesse.php.

6   C. Everett Koop and Francis Schaeffer, *Whatever Hap-
    pened to the Human Race?*, (Westchester, IL: Crossway
    Books, 1979), 36.

7   W. Peacock, "Active Voluntary Euthanasia," *Issues in Law
    and Medicine*, 1987. Cited in John Willke, *Abortion Ques-
    tions and Answers* (Cincinnati, OH: Hayes Publishing,
    1988), 212.

8   S. E. Smith, "Devaluing the Disabled Body," *This Ain't
    Livin'*, August 17, 2009, http://meloukhia.net/2009/08
    /devaluing_the_disabled_body.html.

9   Curtis Young, *The Least of These* (Chicago, IL: Moody
    Press, 1983), 118.

10 Marc A. Thiessen, "When will we stop killing humans with
    Down syndrome?" *The Washington Post*, 8 March 2018,
    https://www.washingtonpost.com/opinions/when-will-we
    -stop-killing-humans-with-down-syndrome/2018/03
    /08/244c9eba-2306-11e8-badd-7c9f29a55815_story.html.

11 Jevan, "People with Down Syndrome Are Happier than
    Normal People," *The Tribal Way* (blog), October 2, 2012,
    http://thetribalway.com/?p=273.

12 H. Choi, M. Van Riper, and S. Thoyre, "Decision Mak-
    ing Following a Prenatal Diagnosis of Down Syndrome:
    An Integrative Review," *Journal of Midwifery and Women's
    Health* 57, no. 2 (March/April 2012): 156–164.

13 Marc A. Thiessen, "When will we stop killing humans with
    Down syndrome?," *The Washington Post*, 8 March 2018,
    https://www.washingtonpost.com/opinions/when-will
    -we-stop-killing-humans-with-down-syndrome/2018/03

/08/244c9eba-2306-11e8-badd-7c9f29a55815_story.html.

14   https://www.youtube.com/watch?v=wkxcoKUupZM

15   https://www.youtube.com/watch?v=7DEUNZifntw

16   https://www.realclearpolitics.com/video/2017/10/31/
     frank_stephens_i_am_a_man_with_down_syndrome
     _and_my_life_is_worth_living.html.

17   Abort73, "Common Abortion Fallacies: Poverty, rape,
     disability, and 'unwantedness' do not morally justify abor-
     tion," accessed January 2, 2020, http://www.abort73.com
     /abortion/common_objections/.

Pro-Choice Claim #11

1   Overpopulation is a Myth, "Episode 1: Overpopulation:
     The Making of a Myth," https://overpopulationisamyth
     .com/overpopulation-the-making-of-a-myth.

2   Eric Holt Gimenez, "We Already Grow Enough Food For
     10 Billion People — and Still Can't End Hunger," *The
     Huffington Post*, May 2, 2012, http://www.huffingtonpost
     .com/eric-holt-gimenez/world-hunger_b_1463429.html.

3   The World Bank, "Fertility rate, total (births per woman),"
     http://data.worldbank.org/indicator/SP.DYN.TFRT.IN?
     locations=US&name_desc=true.

4   U.S. and World Population Clock, December 20, 2019,
     https://www.census.gov/popclock/.

5   Jynnah Radford, "Key findings about U.S. immigrants,"
     Pew Research Center, June 17, 2019, https://www.pew
     research.org/fact-tank/2019/06/17/key-findings-about-u-s
     -immigrants/.

6   Abort73.com, "Common Abortion Fallacies," accessed
     June 1, 2020, http://abort73.com/abortion/common
     _objections.

7   Justin Worland, "How 4 Other Countries Are Trying to
     Get People to Make Babies," *Time*, October 29, 2015,
     http://time.com/4092915/one-child-china-aging/.

8   Colin Mason, "Celebrate 7 Billion People With Us,"
     Christian News Wire, October 19, 2011, http://www.
     christiannewswire.com/news/2632818048.html.

9   Robert Smith, "When Governments Pay People To Have Babies," National Public Radio, November 3, 2011, http://www.npr.org/sections/money/2011/11/03/141943008/when-governments-pay-people-to-have-babies.

10   Veronique de Rugy, "How Many Workers Support One Social Security Retiree?," Mercatus Center, May 22, 2012, https://www.mercatus.org/publications/government-spending/how-many-workers-support-one-social-security-retiree.

11   Ibid.

12   See my book *Does the Birth Control Pill Cause Abortions?* (Read the complete book online at www.epm.org/bcp.)

Pro-Choice Claim #12

1   Martin Luther King Jr., *Strength to Love* (New York: William Collins and World Publishing, 1963), 33.

2   Joy Herndon, M.S., et al, "Abortion Surveillance—United States, 1998," *Morbidity and Mortality Weekly Report (MMWR)*, Centers for Disease Control and Prevention, 7 June 2002.

3   National Right to Life, "Abortion Statistics: United States Data & Trends," http://www.nrlc.org/uploads/factsheets/FS01AbortionintheUS.pdf.

4   The Guttmacher Institute, "Induced Abortion in the United States," September 2019, https://www.guttmacher.org/fact-sheet/induced-abortion-united-states.

5   Bernard Nathanson, MD, *Aborting America,* (New York: Doubleday, 1979), 193.

6   Rethinking Education About Life [REAL], UC San Diego, "Abortion Statistics," http://realweb.ifastnet.com/stats.html.

7   Bernard Nathanson, MD, *Aborting America*, (New York: Doubleday, 1979), 42.

8   "Abortion: For Survival," a video produced by the Fund for the Feminist Majority.

9   Hani K. Atrash, M.D., Theodore Cheek, M.D., and Carol
    Hogue, Ph.D., "Legal Abortion Mortality and General
    Anesthesia," *American Journal of Obstetrics and Gynecology,*
    February 1988, 420.

10 "Jury Orders Abortionist to Pay $25 Million Judgment,"
    Life Advocate, June 1991, 25.

11 Ben Johnson, "8 women, including Gosnell victim, died
    from legal abortion in 2009: Govt report," *Life Site News,*
    December 2, 2013, https://www.lifesitenews.com/news
    /8-women-including-gosnell-victim-died-from-legal
    -abortion-in-2009-govt-repo.

12 Claire Chretien, "Woman dies after late-term abortion at
    shady clinic with history of abuse," *Life Site News,* August
    23, 2017, https://www.lifesitenews.com/news/23-year-old
    -dies-after-late-term-abortion-at-facility-under-criminal
    -invest.

13 Cheryl Sullenger, "Woman enters scandal-plagued Ohio
    facility for abortion, dead next day," *Life Site News,* Sep-
    tember 3, 2019, https://www.lifesitenews.com/news
    /woman-enters-scandal-plagued-ohio-facility-for-abortion
    -dead-next-day.

14 Sarah Kiff, "The Gosnell case: Here's what you need to
    know," *The Washington Post,* April 15, 2013, https://www.
    washingtonpost.com/news/wonk/wp/2013/04/15
    /the-gosnell-case-heres-what-you-need-to-know/.

15 Sarah Ruiz, "Abortion is bad for women's health. Here's
    why.," *Life Site News,* March 18, 2019, https://www.life
    sitenews.com/opinion/why-abortion-is-bad-for-womens
    -health.

Pro-Choice Claim #13

1   Francis J. Beckwith, *Politically Correct Death: Answering
    the Arguments for Abortion Rights* (Grand Rapids, MI:
    Baker Book House, 1993), 87.

2   Abort73.com, "Making a Person Property," Loxafamosity
    Ministries, accessed June 1, 2020, https://abort73.com

/abortion/systematic_injustice/making_a_person
_property/.

Pro-Choice Claim #14

1   Nathan Apodaca, "Are Pro-Lifers Inconsistent, Hypocriti-
     cal, Fetus-Obsessed Jerks?," Life Training Institute, March
     10, 2019, https://prolifetraining.com/are-pro-lifers
     -inconsistent-hypocritical-fetus-obsessed-jerks/.

2   Kyle Blanchette, "No, pro-lifers are not merely pro-birth,"
     The Washington Examiner, May 25, 2019, https://www.
     washingtonexaminer.com/opinion/op-eds/no-pro-lifers
     -are-not-merely-pro-birth.

3   Ardee Coolidge, "Three Myths of the Pro-Life Movement
     Exposed," Care Net, May 17, 2016, https://www.care-net.
     org/abundant-life-blog/three-myths-of-the-pro-life
     -movement-exposed.

Pro-Choice Claim #15

1   For an excellent refutation of the various "Christian" pro-
     choice arguments, see philosophy professor Francis Beck-
     with's "A Critical Appraisal of Theological Arguments
     for Abortion Rights," *Bibliotheca Sacra,* July–September
     1991, 337–55.

2   Virginia Ramey Mollenkott, "Reproductive Choice: Basic
     to Justice for Women," *Christian Scholar's Review,* March
     1988, 291.

3   James Hoffmeier, *Abortion: A Christian Understanding and
     Response* (Grand Rapids, MI: Baker Book House, 1987), 46,
     50; Eugene Quay, "Abortion: Medical and Legal Founda-
     tions," *Georgetown Law Review,* 1967, 395, 420; Meredith
     G. Kline, *"Lex Talionis* and the Human Fetus," *Journal of the
     Evangelical Theological Society,* September 1977, 200–201.

4   Lawrence O. Richards, *Expository Dictionary of Bible
     Words* (Grand Rapids, MI: Zondervan, 1985), 156–57.

5   James Hoffmeier, *Abortion, A Christian Understanding
     and Response* (Grand Rapids, MI: Baker Book House,
     1987), 62.

6 John Jefferson Davis, *Abortion and the Christian* (Phillipsburg, NJ: Presbyterian & Reformed, 1984), 52.

7 Meredith G. Kline, *"Lex Talionis* and the Human Fetus," *Journal of the Evangelical Theological Society,* September 1977, 193.

8 *A Pro-choice Bible Study* (Seattle, WA: Episcopalians for Religious Freedom, 1989).

9 See footnote on Numbers 5:11-31 , *ESV Study Bible* (Wheaton, IL: Crossway Bibles, 2008).

10 Got Questions, "If God hates abortion, why does He allow miscarriages?," accessed January 13, 2020, https://www.gotquestions.org/abortion-miscarriage.html.

11 James Hoffmeier, *Abortion, A Christian Understanding and Response* (Grand Rapids, MI: Baker Book House, 1987), 53.

12 See George Grant, *Grand Illusions: The Legacy of Planned Parenthood* (Brentwood, TN: Wolgemuth & Hyatt, 1988), 190–91.

13 Quoted in Michael Gorman, *Abortion and the Early Church* (Downers Grove, IL: InterVarsity, 1982), 9.

14 John Calvin, *Commentary on Pentateuch,* cited in *Crisis Pregnancy Center Volunteer Training Manual* (Washington, DC: Christian Action Council, 1984), 7.

15 Dietrich Bonhoeffer, *Ethics* (New York: Macmillan, 1955), 131.

16 Karl Barth, *Church Dogmatics,* ed. Geoffrey Bromiley (Edinburgh: T. & T. Clark, 1961), 3:415, 3:418.

Conclusion

1 https://abort73.com/

2 https://pregnancydecisionline.org/find-a-pregnancy-center

3 Sidewalk Advocates for Life, "Frequently Asked Questions," accessed January 13, 2020, https://sidewalkadvocates.org/faqs/.

4 Abort73, "U.S. Abortion Statistics," January 20, 2017, http://www.abort73.com/abortion_facts/us_abortion_statistics.

5   For more on this subject see: http://www.epm.org/bcp.

Appendix

1   Margaret Sanger, *Pivot of Civilization* (New York: Brentano's, 1922), 176.
2   Ibid., 177.
3   Ibid., 112, 116.
4   Ibid., 113.
5   Ibid., 115.
6   Havelock Ellis, "The World's Racial Problem," Birth Control Review (BCR), October 1920, 14–16; Theodore Russell Robie, "Toward Race Betterment," BCR, April 1933, 93–95; Ernst Rudin, "Eugenic Sterilization: An Urgent Need," BCR, April 1933, 102–4.
7   C. O. McCormick, "Defective Families," *Birth Control Review,* April 1933, 98.
8   Dr. Havelock Ellis, "Birth Control and Sterilization," *Birth Control Review,* April 1933, 104.
9   Marvin Olasky, *Abortion Rites: A Social History of Abortion in America* (Wheaton, IL: Crossway Books, 1992), 259.
10 Sanger, *Pivot of Civilization*, 116–7.
11 The Guttmacher Institute, "Abortion rates by race and ethnicity," October 19, 2017, https://www.guttmacher.org/infographic/2017/abortion-rates-race-and-ethnicity.
12 BlackGenocide.org, accessed May 29, 2020, http://www.blackgenocide.org/black.html.
13 Nikita Stewart, "Planned Parenthood in N.Y. Disavows Margaret Sanger Over Eugenics," *The New York Times*, July 21, 2020, https://www.nytimes.com/2020/07/21/nyregion/planned-parenthood-margaret-sanger-eugenics.html.